Longman Stud...

Fire the Sun

Modern Women Writers

Series editor: Maura Healy

The *Modern Women Writers* series is part of the
Longman Study Texts   General editor: Richard Adams

Fire the Sun

An anthology of poems

edited by
Maura Healy

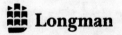
Longman

Longman Group UK Limited,
Longman House, Burnt Mill, Harlow,
Essex CM20 2JE, England
and Associated Companies throughout the world.

First published 1989

Set in 10/12 point Baskerville Linotron
Produced by Longman Group (FE) Ltd
Printed in Hong Kong

ISBN 0 582 02514 1

For Laurie, Tom and baby Jack

Contents

Introduction

Why make a collection of women's poems? Because there are
so many fine poems to be read. Because they don't appear in
school anthologies, by and large, and this means that women's
voices are not often heard in our classrooms. Their experience
and their perspective is undervalued or invisible.

You can find the odd poem by a woman in school anthol-
ogies. It's usually by Sylvia Plath or Stevie Smith – both great
writers. But for many editors it seems that the 'token' woman
writer is enough. No further search is needed to find more
women poets. Anthologies selected for adult readers mostly
follow the same pattern. For some reason women writers are
not considered. It certainly is not because they are not good
enough; this anthology contains many superb poems. We can
only guess at reasons. This is what Jeni Couzyn, poet and
editor of *The Bloodaxe Book of Contemporary Women Poets*, has to
say:

> Poetry .... is read for pleasure only by a very few. It is
> mainly valued (by our society) as the castor oil of education
> – that which one 'didn't much care for at school but was
> forced to learn', and no child would be considered educated
> in our society unless it had been forced to swallow some of
> the unpleasant stuff. It is considered good for growing
> minds, as milk is good for young bodies, but only the
> strongest mental athletes expect to go on taking it after they
> grow up.
>
> Therefore, it is the educators, the critics, the academics
> and the editors and publishers who have given poets repu-
> tations and these are all male dominated ... professions.

She believes, then, that it is men who decide which poets are
great and which should be studied and that they don't give
equal value to women poets.

It is impossible to separate this from the role of women in society and from the value we give to what women have to say. We have a whole vocabulary to criticise women's talk. We don't have the equivalent words for what men say. They exchange information while women gossip. They repeat instructions while women nag. It's hard for women to be confident that what they have to say is worth hearing, worth publishing. They don't see many other women's poems being published and that might even confirm their doubts.

In the last ten years. new publishers have started to promote women's writing both here and in America. There has been a huge and exciting growth in women's literature available for us to read and enjoy. One publishing group, Virago, paved the way. They were joined by The Women's Press and suddenly many smaller publishing houses were set up. Women's writing is now big business. Almost all bookshops will now have their women's section, and publishers have tried to ensure that they promote some women writers.

It's hard to say whether women's poems have a different subject matter from those of men. Of course they describe different experiences from those of men. For example, men don't give birth and this anthology contains some excellent poems about pregnancy and birth which could only have been written by women. Some of the poems here are about rearing children and running a home. Many celebrate the strength of mothers and grandmothers. Margaret Walker's poem 'Lineage' (page 106) is an example:

My grandmothers were strong.
They followed plows and bent to toil.
They moved through fields sowing seed.
They touched earth and grain grew.
They were full of sturdiness and singing.
My grandmothers were strong.

Some of them are about love, but they are not sentimental.

These women are not passively waiting for Mr Wonderful to sweep them off their feet. Grace Nichol's poem 'Even Tho' (page 26) is an example:

Man I love
but won't let you devour

even tho
I'm all watermelon
and star-apple and plum
when you touch me

Sometimes these topics are seen as women's issues. The things women write about are important for all of us. If they focus on issues to do with birth, loving, ageing and death, it is because these are universal issues. The poems in this collection make us think hard about our life and our society. A good poem should 'pull you up short' and make you think again about something you thought you understood or open your mind to a whole new experience or way of thinking about things. As Merle Collins tells us in 'No Dialects Please' (page 7) 'poetry of worth' can 'wrap up a feelin/and fling it back hard'.

Often the poems surprise us because of the strength of feeling they express. Many of the strongest poems in this collection are written by black women. Their voices are raised in anger and in celebration, 'like a woman undaunted' (page 102), as Alice Walker expresses it. And the anthology brings together the experiences of women in joy, in pain, in everyday life – surviving it undaunted.

The poems have been grouped into nine sections. The sections are only there to help the reader focus on key themes or issues. They are to be read, preferably aloud, and enjoyed.

Maura Healy

Before you start reading

These poems should 'speak for themselves'. They have been carefully chosen for GCSE students. Some are much simpler than others but none should be too complicated for you to enjoy reading. Good poems should make you think and should be worth reading over and over again.

The way we read poems is different from the way we read other things. Each word in a poem is very carefully chosen, the patterns that the words make – the rhyme and rhythm are carefully chosen. Part of the joy of reading poems is in admiring the skilful choices of the poet, how she matches what she has to say with the way she says it. Poetry is meant to be read out loud. That way we enjoy the patterns more.

Learning to read poetry

When you settle down to read new poems, here are some things you can do to enjoy them to the full:

1 *Relax.*

Don't think poetry *has* to be difficult. You will need to puzzle over some of these poems, but a poem that doesn't make sense to you after you have read it really carefully is either a poor poem or one that you should return to when you are older and more experienced in reading poems.

The poet *wants* you to understand what she has to say. She has written the poem to share an important idea, experience or emotion. So let the poem 'speak to you'.

2 *Look at the title.*
Think about what it tells you.

3 *Quickly read the whole poem.*
Jot down or discuss with a friend what you think it is about

and whether it appeals to you or not. Give it a second chance, even if you don't like it at first.

4 *Read it again more slowly.*
Think carefully about what the poet is saying.

5 *Read it out loud.*
When you do this you will find that the meanings will begin to emerge.

Let the patterns in the poem emerge as you read out loud. Pause briefly at the end of each line and use the punctuation to allow you to follow the poet's sentences. A good poem to read out loud is 'How Poems Are Made/A Discredited View' on pages 5–6. Just follow Alice Walker's rhythms in the second verse as you read it aloud:

These lines have the same rhythm. { There is a place the fear must go. } Pause at full stop.
There is a place the choice
  must go.
} Pause at full stop.
There is a place the loss must go. } Pause at full stop.
The leftover love. } short sharp line
The love that spills out } These lines run into
of the too full cup } each other smoothly.
and runs and hides } like water pouring
its too full self } out of the cup
in shame.   a short sharp line
          to make a point.

6 *Let the sound of the words emerge.*
'I'm in here hiding', the first poem in the anthology, is a good one to try to do this with.

    I'm in here hiding from words.
    they *cloud* my *vision* like *wide-winged birds.*

When you read the words in italics let them lengthen themselves like those birds stretching their wide wings.

> Some *darker* ones *harsh* and *crowlike*
> *picking issues* to barebone.

Make these words sound harsh and sharp like the birds pecking. You will see how the poet uses the sound of her words to share her emotion with you.

7 *Let the verse structure help you.*

When a poet uses verses it is to mark new ideas or development in her ideas. 'Taint' by Grace Nichols (page 103) is a good example of this:

But I was stolen by men the colour of my own skin borne away by men whose heels had become hoofs whose hands had turned talons bearing me down 　　to the trail of darkness	*Verse 1* tell us how she was captured.
But I was traded by men the colour of my own skin traded like a fowl like a goat like a sack of kernels I was traded 　　for beads　for pans for trinkets?	*Verse 2* tell us how she was sold into slavery.
No it isn't easy to forget what we refuse to remember	*Verse 3* tells us how the memory haunts her.
Daily I rinse the taint of treachery from my mouth	*Verse 4* The sense of betrayal, like a foul taste in her mouth, is daily rinsed out only to return.

8 *Notice if she repeats lines or echoes her words.*

Grace Nichols does this in 'Taint'. One of the most painful things for her was being stolen and traded by black men. The repetition emphasises her pain.

Alice Walker does this in 'How Poems Are Made/A Discredited View (pages 5–6):

> There is a place the fear must go.
> There is a place the choice must go.
> There is a place the loss must go.

The place is a poem. Alice Walker is writing about the emotions and experiences that are the ingredients of poetry. The poem ends with another repetition:

> There is a place the loss must go.
> There is a place the gain must go.
> The leftover love.

Above all, then, it is what is left over from love – the fear, the loss, the gains, the choices we make, that make up our poems. The repetition highlights the idea and presents it to us as her discovery as to how poems are made.

9 *Notice the images the poets use.*

Merle Collins in 'No Dialects Please' (page 7) says that 'poetry of worth' 'could wrap up a feelin/and fling it back hard'.

Imagery is a kind of wrapping up and flinging back of feelings or experiences, and good images hit us hard. They strike us with their freshness, vividness and power. There are many, many images to enjoy in this anthology. Look, for example, at Margaret Atwood's poem 'Dream 2: Brian The Still-hunter' (page 54). He was a man who had to kill

but every time I aim, I feel
my skin grow fur
my head heavy with antlers
and during the stretched instant
the bullet glides on its thread of speed
my soul runs innocent as hooves.

He imagines he is the deer he hunts.

The moment between firing and the kill seems to last a long time.

The bullet moves easily and directly to the target like a bead on a thread.

For that moment he is as pure and innocent as the hooves of the deer trying to escape death.

Grace Nichols uses powerful images in 'Even Tho' (page 26):

Man I love
but won't let you devour

even tho
I'm all watermelon
and star-apple and plum
when you touch me

She becomes soft and yielding like a sweet ripe fruit in his arms but she is not prepared to be eaten by him, devoured or dominated by him.

10 *Look out for rhyme patterns.*

These vary a great deal. Some poems, like 'Rondeau Redoublé' (page 35) by Wendy Cope have a very clear rhyme pattern:

There are so many kinds of awful men –
One can't avoid them all. She often said
She'd never make the same mistake again:
She'd always make a new mistake instead.

In this case the rhyme gives you a sense that you can guess what's coming next – another awful man. The pattern of the rhymes is like the pattern of the woman's life. The poet uses the pattern to 'act out' during the poem the repetition of disasters in the woman's life. The rhythm and rhyme are like a nursery rhyme and somehow this gives the story of this sad woman a 'bitter-sweet' feel.

Another poem which uses rhyme to create a strange effect is Stevie Smith's 'Not Waving but Drowning' (page 42).

Nobody heard him, the dead man,
But still he lay moaning:
I was much further out than you thought
And not waving but drowning.

Poor chap, he always loved larking
And now he's dead
It must have been too cold for him his heart gave way
They said.

Oh no no no, it was too cold always
(Still the dead one lay moaning)
I was much too far out all my life
And not waving but drowning.

There are several poems in this anthology which use very elaborate patterns of rhyme and rhythm. Anne Sexton's 'Elizabeth Gone' (page 98) is a good example. The poem is about Elizabeth's death and this is the first verse.

You lay in the nest of your real **death**,
Beyond the print of my nervous fingers
Where they touched your moving **head**;
Your old skin puckering, your lung's **breath**
Grown baby short as you looked up last
At my face swinging over the human **bed**,
And somewhere you cried, *let me go let me go*.

The rhyme pattern (shown in dark type) in the first six lines is quite tight. It holds the lines together, just as the poet is trying with her 'nervous fingers' to keep Elizabeth from death. In the last line we see Elizabeth trying to escape from life. The line escapes the rhyme pattern. It is longer than the others too, breaking the rhythm pattern of the rest of the verse, escaping from that too. In this way Anne Sexton uses the sound patterns of her poem to develop and express the idea she is exploring.

11 *Develop your own skills.*
'Imitation is the sincerest form of flattery.' If you like an idea or a technique a poet uses, try to build it into your own writing. The more experience you have of different styles and subject matter the better. You will then be able to develop your own poetry in which your own voice can be clearly heard.

Fire the Sun

An anthology of poems

I'm in here hiding from words

I'm In Here Hiding

I'm in here hiding from words
they cloud my vision like wide-winged birds.
Some darker ones harsh and crowlike
picking issues to barebone.
I've shut my doors against them before
but they've come tapping at back doors
or highpains of windows
screaming to be let in,
to cover quieter conversations
with feathers and droppings.

Lorna Goodison

How Poems Are Made/A Discredited View

Letting go
in order to hold on
I gradually understand
how poems are made.

There is a place the fear must go.
There is a place the choice must go.
There is a place the loss must go.
The leftover love.
The love that spills out
of the too full cup
and runs and hides
its too full self
in shame.

I gradually comprehend
how poems are made.
To the upbeat flight of memories.
The flagged beats of the running
heart.

I understand how poems are made.
They are the tears
that season the smile.
The stiff-neck laughter
that crowds the throat.
The leftover love.

I know how poems are made.

There is a place the loss must go.
There is a place the gain must go.
The leftover love.

Alice Walker

No Dialects Please

In this competition
dey was lookin for poetry of worth
for a writin that could wrap up a feelin
an fling it back hard
with a captive power to choke de stars
so dey say,
'Send them to us
but NO DIALECTS PLEASE'
We're British!

Ay!
Well ah laugh till me boushet near drop
Is not only dat ah tink
of de dialect of de Normans and de Saxons
dat combine an reformulate
to create a language-elect
is not only dat ah tink
how dis British education mus really be narrow
if it leave dem wid no knowledge
of what dey own history is about
is not only dat ah tink
bout de part of my story
dat come from Liverpool in a big dirty white
ship mark
AFRICAN SLAVES PLEASE!
We're the British!

But as if dat not enough pain
for a body to bear
ah tink bout de part on de plantations down dere

Wey dey so frighten o de power
in the deep spaces
behind our watching faces
dat dey shout
NO AFRICAN LANGUAGES PLEASE!
It's against the law!
Make me ha to go
an start up a language o me own
dat ah could share wid me people

Den when we start to shout
bout a culture o we own
a language o we own
a identity o we own
dem an de others dey leave to control us say
STOP THAT NONSENSE NOW
We're all British!
Every time we lif we foot to do we own ting
to fight we own fight
dey tell us how British we British
an ah wonder if dey remember
dat in Trinidad in the thirties
dey jail Butler
who dey say is their British citizen
an accuse him of
Hampering the war effort!
Then it was
FIGHT FOR YOUR COUNTRY, FOLKS!
You're British!

Ay! Ay!
Ah wonder when it change to
NO DIALECTS PLEASE!

WE'RE British!
Huh!
To tink how still dey so dunce
an so frighten o we power
dat dey have to hide behind a language
that we could wrap roun we little finger
in addition to we own!
Heavens o mercy!
Dat is dunceness oui!
Ah wonder where is de bright British?

Merle Collins

'Silence is Nearer to Truth'

I handed my teacher a poem,
'This is not a poem,' he said.
'It has no form,
Your lines are unpoetic.
Silence is nearer to truth
Than your written thoughts are to verse.'
Feeling I had betrayed my learning
I laboured through the years to perfect my style
Wishing for the day when my teacher
Would recognise me as a poet.
Now I have little conversation left
I wonder if I handed this poem to him
Would my teacher clasp me to his breast
Or would he send me backwards in my craft
With the proclamation:
'Silence is nearer to truth
Than your written thoughts are to verse.'

                                        Margot Jordan

Stillborn

These poems do not live: it's a sad diagnosis.
They grew their toes and fingers well enough,
Their little foreheads bulged with concentration.
If they missed out on walking about like people
It wasn't for any lack of mother-love.

O I cannot understand what happened to them!
They are proper in shape and number and every part.
They sit so nicely in the pickling fluid!
They smile and smile and smile and smile at me.
And still the lungs won't fill and the heart won't start.

They are not pigs, they are not even fish,
Though they have a piggy and a fishy air –
It would be better if they were alive, and that's what
    they were.
But they are dead, and their mother near dead with
    distraction,
And they stupidly stare, and do not speak of her.

Sylvia Plath

We the women

We the Women

We the women who toil
unadorn
heads tie with cheap
cotton

We the women who cut
clear fetch dig sing

We the women making
something from this
ache-and-pain-a-me
back-o-hardness

Yet we the women
who praises go unsung
who voices go unheard
who deaths they sweep
aside
as easy as dead leaves

Grace Nichols

It Must

Friends, sisters, are you used to your face in the mirror?
Can you accept or even recognise it?
Don't be angry, answer me frankly, excuse
the question's crudity. I can't – no matter
how often I take the little square of glass
from my bag, or furtively glance into shop-windows,
the face reflected back is always a shock.

Those scars and wrinkles, the clumping of pigment
into moles, spots, faulty warty growths
around hairline and neck, the way skin's texture changes
absolutely, becomes roughened and scaly,
coarse-grained, every pore visible, as though
the magnification were intensified: horrible.
These days, I prefer firmer flesh in close-up.

Younger, I remember how I stared, with a mixture
of attraction, repulsion, and pity, at the cheeks of older
women – the sort I chose for friends. Did they
need me as much as I idealized them?
There seemed something splendid and brave about such
   raddled
features, crusted and blurred with the same heavy make-up
I've taken to wearing – warpaint, if, as they say,
the real function of warpaint is to bolster
the uncertain warrior's spirit, more than to
undermine and terrify his opponent.

Now, I long to ask my friends these very
questions and compare reactions, blurt out
the taboo words. But we're so polite, so lavish
with compliments, tender, protective – cherishing
the common hurt: tenderness of bruised flesh,
darkness under the eyes from held-back tears,
watery blisters on frost-touched fruit already
decaying, marked by death's irregularities.

Friends, tell me the truth. Do you also
sometimes feel a sudden jaunty indifference,
or even better, extraordinary moments
when you positively welcome the new
face that greets you from the mirror like
a mother – not your own mother, but that other
dream-figure of she-you-always-yearned-for.
Your face, if you try, can become hers. It must.

Ruth Fainlight

House of Changes

My body is a wide house
a commune
of bickering women, hearing
their own breathing
denying each other.

Nearest the door
ready in her black leather
is *Vulnerable*. She lives in the hall
her face painted with care
her black boots reaching her crotch
her black hair shining
her skin milky and soft as butter.
If you should ring the doorbell
she would answer
and a wound would open across her eyes
as she touched your hand.

On the stairs, glossy and determined
is *Mindful*. She's the boss, handing out
punishments and rations and examination
papers with precise
justice. She keeps her perceptions in a huge
album under her arm
her debts in the garden with the weedkill
friends in a card-index
on the windowsill of the sittingroom
and a tape-recording of the world
on earphones
which she plays to herself over and over
assessing her life
writing summaries.

In the kitchen is *Commendable*.
The only lady in the house who
dresses in florals
she is always busy, always doing something
for someone she has
a lot of friends. Her hands are quick and
cunning as blackbirds
her pantry is stuffed with loaves and fishes
she knows the times of trains and
mends fuses and makes
a lot of noise with the vacuum cleaner.
In her linen cupboard, new-ironed and neatly
folded, she keeps her resentments like
wedding presents – each week
takes them out for counting not to
lose any but would never think of
using any being a lady.

Upstairs in a white room is
my favourite. She is *Equivocal*
has no flesh on her bones
that are changeable as yarrow stalks.
She hears her green plants talking
watches the bad dreams under the world
unfolding
spends all her days and nights
arranging her symbols
never sleeps
never eats hamburgers
never lets anyone into her room
never asks for anything.

In the basement is *Harmful*.
She is the keeper of weapons
the watchdog. Keeps intruders at bay
but the others keep her
locked up in the daytime and when she escapes
she comes out screaming
smoke streaming from her nostrils
flames on her tongue
razor-blades for fingernails
skewers for eyes.

I am *Imminent*
live out in the street
watching them. I lodge myself in other people's
heads with a sleeping bag
strapped to my back.
One day I'll perhaps get to like them enough
those rough, truthful women
to move in. One by one
I'm making friends with them all
unobtrusively, slow and steady
slow and steady.

                              Jeni Couzyn

The Woman in the Ordinary

The woman in the ordinary pudgy downcast girl
is crouching with eyes and muscles clenched.
Round and pebble smooth she effaces herself
under ripples of conversation and debate.
The woman in the block of ivory soap
has massive thighs that neigh,
great breasts that blare and strong arms that trumpet.
The woman of the golden fleece
laughs uproariously from the belly
inside the girl who imitates
a Christmas card virgin with glued hands,
who fishes for herself in others' eyes,
who stoops and creeps to make herself smaller.
In her bottled up is a woman peppery as curry,
a yam of a woman of butter and brass,
compounded of acid and sweet like a pineapple,
like a handgrenade set to explode,
like goldenrod ready to bloom.

Marge Piercy

Three Poems for Women

1   This is a poem for a woman doing dishes.
This is a poem for a woman doing dishes.
It must be repeated.
It must be repeated,
again and again,
again and again,
because the woman doing dishes
because the woman doing dishes
has trouble hearing
has trouble hearing.

2   And this is another poem for a woman
cleaning the floor
who cannot hear at all.
Let us have a moment of silence
for the woman who cleans the floor.

3   And here is one more poem
for the woman at home
with children.
You never see her at night.
Stare at an empty space and imagine her there,
the woman with children
because she cannot be here to speak
for herself,
and listen
to what you think
she might say.

Susan Griffin

21

Ye Housewyf

Ther was a housewyf, strong and coarse of hände,
Who loved the sink the least in all the lands.
A coverchief hadde she upon hir head
Fetis it were and eek of scarlet reed,
Lank hänge hir lockès, straight and blonde of hewe,
For she usèd peroxide, and this is trewe,
And lo! Somethyne to shock the toun,
Hänged from hir fulle red lippës doun
A cygarette, of brande Woodbyne,
Filtre-tipped, and of tobacco fyne.
   Whenne she hadde prepared her husbande's tea,
Chippës fyne, and fisher fingers three,
Hastily sped she hither to the toun,
For Byngo loved she mo than anythynge.
For all thes faults, wel coude she carp and synge.

Meg Wanless

To Friends

I climbed those thoughts with grappling hooks,
Testing the way as I went.
And when I came to an understanding,
The smoothness of the path made me wonder.
How come I hadn't slid down?

And then I remembered the fine, glinting vision-threads
Spinning between us all.
How we made our bodies into little rocks and boulders
For each other to grip and rest on
While the going was bad.

Anna Dolezal

Like a wild iris in the fields

Love Should Grow Up
Like a Wild Iris in the Fields

Love should grow up like a wild iris in the fields,
unexpected, after a terrible storm, opening a purple
mouth to the rain, with not a thought to the future,
ignorant of the grass and the graveyard of leaves
around, forgetting its own beginning. Love should
grow like a wild iris
but does not.
Love more often is to be found in kitchens at the dinner
hour,
tired out and hungry, lingers over tables in houses where
the walls record movements; while the cook is probably
angry,
and the ingredients of the meal are budgeted, while
a child cries feed me now and her mother is not quite
hysterical says over and over, wait just a bit, just a bit,
love should grow up in the fields like a wild iris
but never does
really startle anyone, was to be expected, was to be
predicted, is almost absurd, goes on from day to day, not
quite
blindly, gets taken to the cleaners every fall, sings old
songs over and over, and falls on the same piece of rug
that
never gets tacked down, gives up, wants to hide, is not
brave, knows too much, is not like an
iris growing wild but more like
staring into space
in the street

not quite sure
which door it was, annoyed about the sidewalk being
slippery, trying all the doors, thinking
if love wished the world to be well, it would be well
Love should
grow up like a wild iris, but doesn't, it comes from
the midst of everything else, sees like the iris
of an eye, when the light is right,
feels in blindness and when there is nothing else is
tender, blinks, and opens
face up to the skies.

Susan Griffin

Even Tho

Man I love
but won't let you devour

even tho
I'm all watermelon
and star-apple and plum
when you touch me

even tho
I'm all sea moss
and jelly fish
and tongue

Come
leh we go to de carnival
You be banana
I be avocado

Come
leh we hug-up
an brace-up
an sweet one another up

But then
leh we break free
yes   leh we break free

an keep to de motion
of we own personality

Grace Nichols

night letter

the telephone company is harassin me in my
sleep   everybody keeps callin
'hello hello'   old lovers i never want to see
lovers i'm dying to meet   'hello hello'
i don't know who to answer
i say who is this/   so i'll know how to talk
to em/   what do you want   i'm sleepin
& everythin you say is a lie/   i'm makin you
up to call in my sleep cuz there are so many
disconnections in the day

say there operator   i need some assistance
i move my hand from my ear   (there is no telephone
in my bed   i am sweaty from the cat's fur
on my face)   there is no one to nestle
in the middle of my dreams
to hold me
everybody goes to a phone in my sleep
to call me up
they love me so much

  DING DONG   DING DONG   DING DONG
the special ring of my dream telephone waz $6.31 a
   month
more than regular service for unlimited local calls

you didnt call at noon
but at dawn in my dream you ring & laugh
cuz all i can make up for you to say is
'do you love me'

conversations with self disguised as you i wd have close
so i wake in the cold oakland fog
my eyes stinging with tears
in the telephone conversation it waz
almost you

you almost admitted not bein able
to leave me alone/ almost said
you wd come across the bridge to me
(& my face is swollen/ red on the right side
where i lean on the metallic telephone wires)
i dont believe you will refuse to keep the engagements
we made inside my sleep
                        thulani is coming for lunch
                 jessica is going to speak to auntie pearl
                         bout my sequins
    conyus is bakin mandarin chickens
& nashira is holdin a plant for me
today i'm gonna go see my friends
who called me up last night in my sleep

it is so   it is real
I cd not hear yr voices so perfect
if yr spirits werent running in the
night air/ in my telephone nightgown i stood
   on the porch
waitin for the one of you sposed
to take me to breakfast
     it is so   it is real
gene quoted a swami in boston
       'visions are messages of those who love us'
& i know you love me cuz everybody
called at the same time

you all called to let me know what you were doin
but when i woke   exhausted from
chattin all night   i go to meet you
& where are you   callin somebody
who can talk in the daytime

this is destroyin in my writin
my dancin suffers from continual interruption
operators makin yr collect calls everywhere i go
'hello hello do you love me   hello hello hello
    stop ringin me up
if you cant remember dreams/ i cant be yr friend
if you dont
keep
the
appointment

you direct yr spirit to make connections/
leave me on the wharf
callin sea gulls

Ntozake Shange

lady in blue

one thing i dont need
is any more apologies
i got sorry greetin me at my front door
you can keep yrs
i dont know what to do wit em
they dont open doors
or bring the sun back
they dont make me happy
or get a mornin paper
didnt nobody stop usin my tears to wash cars
cuz a sorry

i am simply tired
of collectin
      'i didnt know
        i was so important toyou'
i'm gonna haveta throw some away
i cant get to the clothes in my closet
for alla the sorries
i'm gonna tack a sign to my door
leave a message by the phone
      'if you called
      to say yr sorry
      call somebody
      else
      i dont use em anymore'
i let sorry/ didnt meanta/ & how cd i know abt that
take a walk down a dark & musty street in brooklyn
i'm gonna do exactly what i want to
& i wont be sorry for none of it
letta sorry soothe yr soul/ i'm gonna soothe mine

you were always inconsistent
doin somethin & then bein sorry
beatin my heart to death
talkin bout you sorry
well
i will not call
i'm not goin to be nice
i will raise my voice
& scream & holler
& break things & race the engine
& tell all yr secrets bout yrself to yr face
& i will list in detail everyone of my wonderful lovers
& their ways
i will play oliver lake
loud
& i wont be sorry for none of it

i loved you on purpose
i was open on purpose
i still crave vulnerability & close talk
& i'm not even sorry bout you bein sorry
you can carry all the guilt & grime ya wanna
just dont give it to me
i cant use another sorry
next time
you should admit
you're mean/ low-down/ triflin/ & no count straight out
steada bein sorry alla the time
enjoy bein yrself

Ntozake Shange

32

Dawn Walkers

Anxious eyes loom down the damp-black streets
Pale staring girls who are walking away hard
From beds where love went wrong or died or turned
    away,
Treading their misery beneath another day
Stamping to work into another morning.

In all our youths there must have been some time
When the cold dark has stiffened up the wind
But suddenly, like a sail stiffening with wind,
Carried the vessel on, stretching the ropes, glad of it.

But listen to this now: this I saw one morning.
I saw a young man running, for a bus I thought,
Needing to catch it on this murky morning
Dodging the people crowding to work or shopping early.
And all heads stopped and turned to see how he ran
To see would he make it, the beautiful strong young
    man.
Then I noticed a girl running after, calling out 'John'.
He must have left his sandwiches I thought.
But she screamed 'John wait'. He heard her and ran
    faster,
Using his muscled legs and studded boots.
We knew she'd never reach him. 'Listen to me John.
Only once more' she cried. 'For the last time, John,
    please wait, please listen.'
He gained the corner in a spurt and she
Sobbing and hopping with her red hair loose

(Made way for by the respectful audience)
Followed on after, but not to catch him now.
Only that there was nothing left to do.

The street closed in and went on with its day.
A worn old man standing in the heat from the baker's
Said 'Surely to God the bastard could have waited'.

Jenny Joseph

Rondeau Redoublé

There are so many kinds of awful men –
One can't avoid them all. She often said
She'd never make the same mistake again:
She always made a new mistake instead.

The chinless type who made her feel ill-bred;
The practised charmer, less than charming when
He talked about the wife and kids and fled –
There are so many kinds of awful men.

The half-crazed hippy, deeply into Zen,
Whose cryptic homilies she came to dread;
The fervent youth who worshipped Tony Benn –
'One can't avoid them all,' she often said.

The ageing banker, rich and overfed,
Who held forth on the dollar and the yen –
Though there were many more mistakes ahead,
She'd never make the same mistake again.

The budding poet, scribbling in his den
Odes not to her but to his pussy, Fred;
The drunk who fell asleep at nine or ten –
She always made a new mistake instead.

And so the gambler was at least unwed
And didn't preach or sneer or wield a pen
Or hoard his wealth or take the Scotch to bed.
She'd lived and learned and lived and learned but then
There are so many kinds.

Wendy Cope

At 3 a.m.

the room contains no sound
except the ticking of the clock
which has begun to panic
like an insect, trapped
in an enormous box.

Books lie open on the carpet.

Somewhere else
you're sleeping
and beside you there's a woman
who is crying quietly
so you won't wake.

Wendy Cope

Moonlongings

Moonlongings

When the full moon blows
She'd get this silver strange
desire to assume gossamer colours
and float through the secrets of trees,
to rest in the womb of a moon.

Sometimes it would be a half wane of a moon
with a sliver of a stoop
ready for her to sit,
trailing her skirts to cover
the heads of sleeping birds.

But the real desire was to use the moon
as a moon vehicle to travel to his window
blowing kisses on his
sleeping face.

She'd leave a sign between the pages
of a poem that gave ways
to catch a bird
and keep it.

Some nights the moon it seemed
would send cobweb invitations
to her eyes.

Come morning
She'd wake from a pillow
sprayed with witches' tears
to find the longing still
floating in the pools of her eyes.

Lorna Goodison

Blue Moles

(1)

They're out of the dark's ragbag, these two
Moles dead in the pebbled rut,
Shapeless as flung gloves, a few feet apart –
Blue suede a dog or fox has chewed.
One, by himself, seemed pitiable enough,
Little victim unearthed by some large creature
From his orbit under the elm root.
The second carcass makes a duel of the affair:
Blind twins bitten by bad nature.

The sky's far dome is sane and clear.
Leaves, undoing their yellow caves
Between the road and the lake water,
Bare no sinister spaces. Already
The moles look neutral as the stones.
Their corkscrew noses, their white hands
Uplifted, stiffen in a family pose.
Difficult to imagine how fury struck –
Dissolved now, smoke of an old war.

(2)

Nightly the battle-shouts start up
In the ear of the veteran, and again
I enter the soft pelt of the mole.
Light's death to them: they shrivel in it.
They move through their mute rooms while I sleep,
Palming the earth aside, grubbers

40

After the fat children of root and rock.
By day, only the topsoil heaves.
Down there one is alone.

Outsize hands prepare a path,
They go before: opening the veins,
Delving for the appendages
Of beetles, sweetbreads, shards – to be eaten
Over and over. And still the heaven
Of final surfeit is just as far
From the door as ever. What happens between us
Happens in darkness, vanishes
Easy and often as each breath.

Sylvia Plath

Not Waving but Drowning

Nobody heard him, the dead man,
But still he lay moaning:
I was much further out than you thought
And not waving but drowning.

Poor chap, he always loved larking
And now he's dead
It must have been too cold for him his heart gave way
They said.

Oh no no no, it was too cold always
(Still the dead one lay moaning)
I was much too far out all my life
And not waving but drowning.

Stevie Smith

Child

Your clear eye is the one absolutely beautiful thing.
I want to fill it with color and ducks,
The zoo of the new

Whose names you meditate –
April snowdrop, Indian pipe,
Little

Stalk without wrinkle,
Pool in which images
Should be grand and classical

Not this troublous
Wringing of hands, this dark
Ceiling without a star.

Sylvia Plath

The planet where they lose things

Lost, Never Found

'That is the place,' said the Astronomer
Leaning from behind Arcturus
In earth's upper sky
'The planet where they lose things,
Where no one can find
Their lost knives, wives, dogs or hogs,
Their money or their lives
Once the desired object vanishes from sight.
I've studied them six million years
Since my promotion to this job.
Look –
All kinds of disappearances:
The crew of the *Marie Celeste*
Is only a splinter of the ships
Boats that went out on business or pleasure
Fishermen rich and poor
In canoes, kayaks, junks
Sailors of triremes
Sailors of submarines
(One lies in a valley
In the mountains of the sea)
Lost and never found.
And not only is the sea
Full of men who failed to answer letters
But consider the desert
Where on one occasion two valuable camels
Were wrongly assumed stolen,
The incident starting a tribal war
And never their bones seen
Or their lost footsteps found.

Children, too, have been one moment
All at play in the garden
And the next have stepped through
A door of air into the unknown.
Jewellery and keys have a way
Of departing for parts undisclosed
Without a message
Or a forwarding address.
Parcels go through the post
To the same destination
And somewhere there is wealth untold
Of all the money vanished
Out of wallets, banks, safes
From double-audited accounts
Of respectable merchant ventures
And other less respectable;
From the widow's purse
The collection plate
And every national treasury.
Computers have helped
To lose as much
As ever disappeared from the granaries
Of Thebes or Alexandria or Rome.
Then the names, the languages,
Even the very shapes of things
– The wheel was invented six times,
But who knows about the other five?
Brooches too have fallen in the grass
During processions and tea-parties
Cricket balls, golf balls, arrows and spears
Abound in the vanished place.
Manuscripts, vases, and the results of examinations
Sometimes a whole dinner service

With the Romanov crest
Or the mark of some potter
Working in a shed near Limoges.
Answers to sums
Have gone from exercise books overnight,
Along with Frisky,
Black and white dog with red collar
Please call Peter Brown.
As for the causes, the feuds,
The important issues of the day
Lost, never found
Under clouds of argument and gunsmoke
Untraceable forever
Even though thirty incidents in Budapest
And two in Vienna, six on an estate
Ten miles from Sarajevo
And eight conversations
Spoken in the Croat language
Have yet to be discovered
In the graveyards of the Somme.
So, too, is the week
Spent on a certain Caribbean island
Where the passionate embrace
Of two mutual strangers
Left behind a nameless son
To start a long tradition
Of unparented offspring.
For children mislay parents
Just as often as the other way around.
The worst is, to my mind,
The friendship that slips through the door
During an idle conversation

Runs down to the bus-station
Buys a one-way ticket
For some unknown location.
And their gods too, their gods
Also disappear from time and mind
Sometimes by force.
Yet every generation wonders
Where dreams come from,
Or those wholly unexpected moments on the road
When the heart flames with sudden gold.'

Jean D'Costa

Two Sketches

for Monica and Alice

1   Hiroshima, 1945

Kasa promises. She walks
carefully all the way back
from the shop.

She has one foot on the step
when the sun slips. Her shadow stops.
She looks up.

The sun
does not fall down
until late in the afternoon.

That is a promise. It has been
given to us.
It is only eight fifteen.

She is bringing a bottle of rice wine.
It is precious.
There will be a celebration.

The house is gone.
Kasa stops. There is a shadow on the step
looking up.

2 Birmingham, 1983

Alice examines the shadow
that lies before her
like a future.

It is fantastic:
an elegant woman dressed in black,
an old one bent over a stick.

Alice stops short.
She is only eight,
but she can just imagine it.

Alice, come on up.
The sun has reached the bottom of the step.
It is quarter past eight.

Tomorrow is
another day. That is a promise.
Come.

Alice forgets her shadow. Carelessly
it hops before her
two steps at a time.

Gillian Allnutt

The Fifth Sense

A 65-year-old Cypriot Greek shepherd, Nicolis Loizou, was wounded
by security forces early today. He was challenged twice; when he
failed to answer, troops opened fire. A subsequent hospital
examination showed that the man was deaf. News Item,
30 December 1957.

Lamps burn all the night
Here, where people must be watched and seen,
And I, a shepherd, Nicolis Loizou,
Wish for the dark, for I have been
Sure-footed in the dark, but now my sight
Stumbles among these beds, scattered white boulders,
As I lean towards my far slumbering house
With the night lying upon my shoulders.

My sight was always good,
Better than others. I could taste wine and bread
And name the field' they spattered when the harvest
Broke. I could coil in the red
Scent of the fox out of a maze of wood
And grass. I could touch mist, I could touch breath.
But of my sharp senses I had only four.
The fifth one pinned me to my death.

The soldiers must have called
The word they needed: Halt. Not hearing it,
I was their failure, relaxed against the winter
Sky, the flag of their defeat.

With their five senses they could not have told
That I lacked one, and so they had to shoot.
They would fire at a rainbow if it had
A colour less than they were taught.

Patricia Beer

Dream 2: Brian the Still-hunter

The man I saw in the forest
used to come to our house
every morning, never said anything;
I learned from the neighbours later
he once tried to cut his throat.

I found him at the end of the path
sitting on a fallen tree
cleaning his gun.

There was no wind;
around us the leaves rustled.

He said to me:
I kill because I have to

but every time I aim, I feel
my skin grow fur
my head heavy with antlers
and during the stretched instant
the bullet glides on its thread of speed
my soul runs innocent as hooves.

Is God just to his creatures?

I die more often than many.

He looked up and I saw
the white scar made by the hunting knife
around his neck.

When I woke
I remembered: he has been gone
twenty years and not heard from

Margaret Atwood

Charivari

'They capped their heads with feathers, masked
their faces, wore their clothes backwards, howled
with torches through the midnight winter

and dragged the black man from his house
to the jolting music of broken
instruments, pretending to each other

it was a joke, until
they killed him. I don't know
what happened to the white bride.'

The American lady, adding she
thought it was a disgraceful piece
of business, finished her tea.

(Note: Never pretend this isn't
part of the soil too, teadrinkers, and inadvertent
victims and murderers, when we come this way

again in other forms, take care
to look behind, within
where the skeleton face beneath

the face puts on its feather mask, the arm
within the arm lifts up the spear:
Resist those cracked

drumbeats. Stop this. Become human.)

                                        Margaret Atwood

Victims

They are ageing now, some dead.
In the third-class suburbs of exile
their foreign accents
continue to condemn them. They should
not have expected more.

They had their time
of blazing across headlines,
welcomes, interviews, placings
in jobs that could not fit,
of being walked round carefully.
One averts the eyes
from horror or miracle equally.

Their faces, common to humankind,
had eyes, lips, noses.
That in itself was grave
seen through such a flame.

The Czech boy, talking,
posturing, desperate to please,
restless as a spastic trying
to confine his twitches
into the normal straitjacket –
what could we do with him?

The neighbours asked him
to children's parties,
being at sixteen a child;
gave him small jobs

having no niche to hold him
whether as icon, inhabitant
or memento mori.
He could not be a person
having once been forced to carry
other children's corpses
to the place of burning.
But when we saw him walk
beside our own children
darkness rose from the pit.
Quickly but carefully
(he must not notice)
we put our bodies
between our children and the Victim.

Absit omen, you gods –
avert the doom,
the future's beckoning flame.

Perhaps he did notice. At last
he went away.

In what backstreet of what city
does he keep silence, unreadable
fading graffito of half-
forgotten obscenity?

Think: such are not to be pitied.
They wear already
a coat of ash seared in.
But our children and their children
have put on, over the years
a delicate cloak of fat.

Judith Wright

The Anti-suffragists

Fashionable women in luxurious homes,
With men to feed them, clothe them, pay their bills,
Bow, doff the hat, and fetch the handkerchief;
Hostess or guest, and always so supplied
With graceful deference and courtesy;
Surrounded by their servants, horses, dogs, –
These tell us they have all the rights they want.

Successful women who have won their way
Alone, with strength their unaided arm,
Or helped by friends, so softly climbing up
By the sweet aid of 'woman's influence';
Successful any way, and caring naught
For any other woman's unsuccess, –
These tell us they have all the rights they want.

Religious women of the feebler sort, –
Not the religion of a righteous world,
A free, enlightened, upward-reaching world,
But the religion that considers life
As something to back out of ! – whose ideal
Is to renounce, submit, and sacrifice,
Counting on being patted on the head
And given a high chair when they get to heaven, –
These tell us they have all the rights they want.

Ignorant women – college-bred sometimes,
But ignorant of life's realities
And principles of righteous government,
And how the privileges they enjoy

59

Were won with blood and tears by those before –
Those they condemn, whose ways they now oppose;
Saying, 'Why not let well enough alone?
Our world is very pleasant as it is,' –
These tell us they have all the rights they want.

And selfish women, – pigs in petticoats, –
Rich, poor, wise, unwise, top or bottom round,
But all sublimely innocent of thought,
And guiltless of ambition, save the one
Deep, voiceless aspiration – to be fed!
These have no use for rights or duties more.
Duties to-day are more than they can meet,
And law insures their right to clothes and food, –
These tell us they have all the rights they want.

And, more's the pity, some good women, too;
Good conscientious women, with ideas;
Who think – or think they think – that women's cause
Is best advanced by letting it alone;
That she somehow is not a human thing,
And not to be helped on by human means,
Just added to humanity – an 'L' –
A wing, a branch, an extra, not mankind, –
These tell us they have all the rights they want.

And out of these has come a monstrous thing,
A strange, down-sucking whirlpool of disgrace,
Women uniting against womanhood,
And using that great name to hide their sin!
Vain are their words as that old king's command
Who set his will against the rising tide.

But who shall measure the historic shame
Of these poor traitors – traitors are they all –
To great Democracy and Womanhood!

Charlotte Perkins Gilman

I Am a Union Woman

I am a union woman,
As brave as I can be;
I do not like the bosses,
And the bosses don't like me.

    Refrain:

Join the NMU,
Come join the NMU

I was raised in old Kentucky,
In Kentucky borned and bred;
And when I joined the union
They called me a Rooshian Red.

When my husband asked the boss for a job
These is the words he said:
"Bill Jackson, I can't work you sir,
Your wife's a Rooshian Red."

This the worst time on earth
That I have ever saw;
To get shot down by gun thugs
And framed up by the law.

If you want to join a union
As strong as one can be,
Join the dear old NMU
And come along with me.

We are many thousand strong
And I am glad to say,
We are getting stronger
And stronger every day.

The bosses ride fine horses
While we walk in the mud;
Their banner is a dollar sign
While ours is striped with blood.

Aunt Molly Jackson

These mother's bones

With Child

Now I am slow and placid, fond of sun,
Like a sleek beast, or a worn one,
No slim and languid girl – not glad
With the windy trip I once had,
But velvet-footed, musing of my own,
Torpid, mellow, stupid as a stone.

You cleft me with your beauty's pulse, and now
Your pulse has taken body. Care not how
The old grace goes, how heavy I am grown,
Big with this loneliness, how you alone
Ponder our love. Touch my feet and feel
How earth tingles, teeming at my heel!
Earth's urge, not mine – my little death, not hers;
And the pure beauty yearns and stirs.

It does not heed our ecstasies, it turns
With secrets of its own, its own concerns,
Toward a windy world of its own, toward stark
And solitary places. In the dark
Defiant even now, it tugs and moans
To be untangled from these mother's bones.

Genevieve Taggard

For a Child Expected

Lovers whose lifted hands are candles in winter,
Whose gentle ways like streams in the easy summer,
Lying together
For secret setting of a child, love what they do,
Thinking they make that candle immortal, those streams
    forever flow,
And yet do better than they know.

So the first flutter of a baby felt in the womb,
Its little signal and promise of riches to come,
Is taken in its father's name;
Its life is the body of his love, like his caress,
First delicate and strange, that daily use
Makes dearer and priceless.

Our baby was to be the living sign of our joy,
Restore to each the other's lost infancy;
To a painter's pillaging eye
Poet's coiled hearing, add the heart we might earn
By the help of love; all that our passion would yield
We put to planning our child.

The world flowed in; whatever we liked we took:
For its hair, the gold curls of the November oak
We saw on our walk;
Snowberries that make a Milky Way in the wood
For its tender hands; calm screen of the frozen flood
For our care of its childhood.

But the birth of a child is an uncontrollable glory;
Cat's cradle of hopes will hold no living baby,
Long though it lay quietly.
And when our baby stirs and struggles to be born
It compels humility: what we began
Is now its own.

For *as the sun that shines through glass*
So Jesus in His Mother was.
Therefore every human creature,
Since it shares in His nature,
In candle-gold passion or white
Sharp star should show its own way of light.
May no parental dread or dream
Darken our darling's early beam:
May she grow to her right powers
Unperturbed by passion of ours.

Anne Ridler

The Abortion

Somebody who should have been born
is gone.

Just as the earth puckered its mouth,
each bud puffing out from its knot,
I changed my shoes, and then drove south.

Up past the Blue Mountains, where
Pennsylvania humps on endlessly,
wearing, like a crayoned cat, its green hair,

its roads sunken in like a grey washboard;
where, in truth, the ground cracks evilly,
a dark socket from which the coal has poured,

Somebody who should have been born
is gone.

the grass as bristly and stout as chives,
and me wondering when the ground would break,
and me wondering how anything fragile survives;

up in Pennsylvania, I met a little man,
not Rumpelstiltskin, at all, at all . . .
he took the fullness that love began.

Returning north, even the sky grew thin
like a high window looking nowhere.
The road was as flat as a sheet of tin,

Somebody who should have been born
is gone.

Yes, woman, such logic will lead
to loss without death. Or say what you meant,
you coward . . . this baby that I bleed.

Anne Sexton

For a Child Born Dead

What ceremony can we fit
You into now? If you had come
Out of a warm and noisy room
To this, there'd be an opposite
For us to know you by. We could
Imagine you in lively mood

And then look at the other side,
The mood drawn out of you, the breath
Defeated by the power of death.
But we have never seen you stride
Ambitiously the world we know.
You could not come and yet you go.

But there is nothing now to mar
Your clear refusal of our world.
Not in our memories can we mould
You or distort your character.
Then all our consolation is
That grief can be as pure as this.

Elizabeth Jennings

Poem to My Daughter

'I think I'm going to have it,'
I said, joking between pains.
The midwife rolled competent
sleeves over corpulent milky arms.
'Dear, you never have it,
we deliver it.'
A judgement years proved true.
Certainly I've never had you

as you still have me, Caroline.
Why does a mother need a daughter?
Heart's needle – hostage to fortune –
freedom's end. Yet nothing's more perfect
than that bleating, razor-shaped cry
that delivers a mother to her baby.
The bloodcord snaps that held
their sphere together. The child,
tiny and alone, creates the mother.

A woman's life is her own
until it is taken away
by a first particular cry.
Then she is not alone
but a part of the premises
of everything there is.
A branch, a tide . . . a war.
When we belong to the world
we become what we are.

Anne Stevenson

Transformation

I see you dart into the world
pearly pink like the inside of a shell
streaked with silver.

Look! Look!
I am shouting with joy, rising up
like a phoenix from my pain

With my eyes I behold you
In the flesh I behold you

So a holy man waking into death
from a life of devotion or
martyrdom in flames

might look into the shining face of god
and see at once
he had never believed.

I see you with my eyes
I see you in glory.

From a tatter of flesh I watch them work.
From a pinnacle of joy.
The placenta, purplish liver meat

sails out of my body like a whale
rubbery hands turn it inside out
hold it up to the light.

The sinewy pulsing cord.
In a haze of peace they cut and stitch
my threaded body like scarlet linen

the midwife chatting comfortably
seated at her work, the needle threaded,
the thimble, the green thread

in and out, in and out.
Then washed and trim in clean sheets
they leave us: mother father child

three folded together.
I see your sleeping face
eyelids crescent lines, lips curled translucent

in stillness like a cowrie shell
whirlpool of your hair. I see you breathe.
In a still pool the moon lies quiet.

                              Jeni Couzyn

Dawn

Of your hand I could say this
a bird poised mid-air in flight
as delicate and smooth.

Of your mouth
a foxglove in its taking
without edges or hurt.

This of your ear
a tiny sea-horse, immortal
sporting in white waves

and of your eye
a place where no one could hide
nothing lurk.

Of your cupped flesh
smooth in my palm
an agate on the sea-shore

of your back and belly
that they command kisses.
And of your feet I would say

they are inquisitive and gay
as squirrels or birds
and so return to your hand

75

and begin my voyage
around your loveliness
again and yet again

as in my arms you lie sleeping.

Jeni Couzyn

Songs For My Son   I

My son cries
the cats answer
I hover over his sleeping
suspended on his milk-stained breath
I live in fear of his hurt, his death.
The fear is real
if I close my eyes when it is at its height
I see him curled man-in-miniature asleep.
I hover over his milk-stained breath
and listen for its rise
every one an assurance that he is alive
and if God bargains
I strike a deal with him,
for his life I owe you something, anything
but please let no harm come to him.
The cat cries
my son answers
his sleep is short
his stomach hurts.

Lorna Goodison

Emperor Baby

Your tiny heavy head
Gossed in ginger gold and red
Worked against my marble breast
Doggedly fetching upstream
Till the veins snaked down bluish-green
And I sat up all night holding you
A weary drunken queen.

At one year a Buddha-king
You make the dead objects dance and sing
Bring grace to carpet fluff and string
See diamonds in the dust
Below the lampshade's brim
Your fingers trace
The connections across my face.

All my days are measured in your hours
Clamped by satin gums
I am sucked dry
Undone by your desires
Hooked to me by your green-sea eyes
Your life is a weight
Passing through me
On a thin line to earth.

                              Jehane Markham

Being There

My child called my name in the street as I rushed past,
   unseeing.
Later I turned, and saw her stricken face,
The one she'll wear when she is old
When in a dream she'll call my name, and I,
Having joined the dead, rush on –
Not as today, turn back
To clasp her in my arms.

Ethel Portnoy

Her Belly

She has a right to have a fat belly,
her belly has borne five children.
They warmed themselves at it,
it was the sun of their childhood.

The five children have gone,
her fat belly remains.
This belly
is beautiful.

Anna 'Swir'

Heirloom

Heirloom

She gave me childhood's flowers,
Heather and wild thyme,
Eyebright and tormentil,
Lichen's mealy cup
Dry on wind-scored stone,
The corbies on the rock,
The rowan by the burn.

Sea-marvels a child beheld
Out in the fisherman's boat,
Fringed pulsing violet
Medusa, sea-gooseberries,
Starfish on the sea-floor,
Cowries and rainbow-shells
From pools on a rocky shore.

Gave me her memories,
But kept her last treasure:
'When I was a lass', she said,
'Sitting among the heather,
'Suddenly I saw
'That all the moor was alive!
'I have told no-one before'.

That was my mother's tale.
Seventy years had gone
Since she saw the living skein
Of which the world is woven,
And having seen, knew all;
Through long indifferent years
Treasuring the priceless pearl.

                              Kathleen Raine

Mama

Mama
today it's my turn
to write you before dawn
I turn over at the third hour
of a day not yet broken
by loud crowing cocks
and birds twittering up
and the sun that set at dusk
is not yet ready to rise.

Today is not the first
I am now a customer to the hour
of three
there's an alarm in my head
that never fails at three
I pull on my trousers
pull over my sweater
and over all
your red tie-and-dye maxi
my socks and my sneakers.
retiring to the table
where I always find
sheets and sheets of scribbling
from mornings past
and I am quite ready to talk
silently on paper
or clattering on the keyboard
of my Corona Smith.

Today for the first time
I remember at fifteen
solving your one complaint of sleeplessness
telling you that insomnia is a
positive sign of ageing.
that I'd read it somewhere.
I recall our nicknaming you
our dearest mother rat
for rattling so early
breaking our sleep.

I now know I must tell you
that sleep is now a slippery thing
daily eluding me, avoiding my very clutch
as boiling okro skips smoothly off the
    spoon.

I am now
like mother like daughter
a regular rattler
me with pen and sheets of paper
you with scissors, machine and cloth
rattling is now fashioning out.

I now see the sameness of
your three score but one
and my one score and five
a restless rattling within
alarmingly motioning body
regularly preceding sunrise.

I know not now
if when I've sent you this
you will wait for when I come
and we can talk past midnight
or you will do your normal bid
and write me at three
a time that now speaks
of this sameness
that I see.

Rita Anyiam-St. John

The Mother

Of course I love them, they are my children.
That is my daughter and this my son.
And this is my life I give them to please them.
It has never been used. Keep it safe. Pass it on.

Anne Stevenson

Pain for a Daughter

Blind with love, my daughter
has cried nightly for horses,
those long-necked marchers and churners
that she has mastered, any and all,
reigning them in like a circus hand –
the excitable muscles and the ripe neck;
tending this summer, a pony and a foal.
She who is too squeamish to pull
a thorn from the dog's paw,
watched her pony blossom with distemper,
the underside of the jaw swelling
like an enormous grape.
Gritting her teeth with love,
she drained the boil and scoured it
with hydrogen peroxide until pus
ran like milk on the barn floor.

Blind with loss all winter,
in dungarees, a ski jacket and a hard hat,
she visits the neighbours' stable,
our acreage not zoned for barns;
they who own the flaming horses
and the swan-whipped thoroughbred
that she tugs at and cajoles,
thinking it will burn like a furnace
under her small-hipped English seat.

Blind with pain she limps home.
The thoroughbred has stood on her foot.
He rested there like a building.
He grew into her foot until they were one.
The marks of the horseshoe printed
into her flesh, the tips of her toes ripped
off like pieces of leather,
three toenails swirled like shells
and left to float in blood in her riding boot.

Blind with fear, she sits on the toilet,
her foot balanced over the washbasin,
her father, hydrogen peroxide in hand,
performing the rites of the cleansing.
She bites on a towel, sucked in breath,
sucked in and arched against the pain,
her eyes glancing off me where
I stand at the door, eyes locked
on the ceiling, eyes of a stranger,
and then she cries . . .
Oh my God, help me!
Where a child would have cried *Mama!*
Where a child would have believed *Mama!*
she bit the towel and called on God
and I saw her life stretch out . . .
I saw her torn in childbirth,
and I saw her, at that moment,
in her own death and I knew that she
knew.

Anne Sexton

For My Mother's Mother

Driving with my mother
from Chicago to Boston,
only ourselves to talk to.
In a snow storm between Buffalo and Syracuse
she told me quietly
how her mother died.

I was eight and Lorraine was four.
Lorraine was a difficult child.
We moved a lot because of Daddy's job
but he had finally promised Mother they would settle.
They built a home in the country
with window seats and flagstone fireplace.
We moved in.
Three weeks later Daddy's company wanted him to
   move again.
He went.
Mother was going to pack and follow.
But Lorraine was a difficult child
and Mother was pregnant again.
She couldn't face moving and having another child
so she went to her mother and aunt.
Grandma Andersen told her something,
gave her something,
I don't know,
from the old country.
It didn't work.
She was sick.
I heard her screams from the next room
but they wouldn't let me go in.
By the time Daddy got home she was dead.

He never knew what happened or how she died.
What do you mean, I asked?
How could he not know?
Didn't he care? Didn't he ask?
They just told him it was a woman's problem.
He never knew. After he died
Grandma Andersen told Lorraine and she told me.
All I remembered was the house
where my mother died
and how she cried
and they finally took Lorraine and me away
so we wouldn't hear.

For two years now
I have heard my mother's mother's screams.
They are all I know of her
they are with me.
I have listened to her screams
as they become my own.
I have lived through her death.
Untold, yet I know how she did it.
She took some poison
when that didn't work
she shoved something up her vagina.
And that worked and she bled
and expelled and was infected
and poisoned and she died.
I have heard her screams of pain
splutter through her clenched teeth
and grow weaker.
I have heard her screams of rage
deep in my chest
as she cursed her husband

and her mother
and Lorraine who was always a difficult child
and herself who could not cope,
who should have been different
or better
or more able to manage these things somehow.

I asked, a year later: what was her name?
Whose?
Your mother, my grandmother,
what was her name?
Judith, she said.
I named my first daughter after my mother.

Judith McDaniel

You can wear terrible shirts and grow more fat

The Second Wife

She knows, being woman, that for him she holds
The space kept for the second blossoming,
Unmixed with dreams, held tightly in the folds
Of the accepted and long-proper thing –
She, duly loved; and he, proud of her looks
Shy of her wit. And of that other she knows
She had a slim throat, a nice taste in books,
And grew petunias in squat garden rows.
Thus knowing all, she feels both safe and strange;
Safe in his life, of which she has a share;
Safe in her undisturbed, cool, equal place,
In the sweet commonness that will not change;
And strange, when, at the door, in the spring air,
She hears him sigh, old Aprils in his face.

                                        Lizette Woodworth

Skins

This pair of skin gloves is sixty-six years old,
mended in places, worn thin across the knuckles.

Snakes get rid of their coverings all at once.
Even those empty cuticles trouble the passer-by.

Counting in seven-year rhythms I've lost nine skins
though their gradual flaking isn't so spectacular.

Holding a book or a pen I can't help seeing
how age crazes surfaces. Well, and interiors?

You ask me to read those poems I wrote in my thirties?
They dropped off several incarnations back.

Judith Wright

Blinis

Tonight as I prepared them,
Puffed, small and dappled brown
As they should have been,
I thought of Baboushka
In the long Parisian afternoons
Flattening the bubbles of flour
with a worn wooden spoon and stirring,
stirring the honey-coloured cream.
I was allowed to whip the egg whites dry
and paint a swirl of butter in the pan.
I don't remember eating them.
Just the stooped, content old lady
So engrossed and certain of her art.
Later, she would take me through
The spotted, curling photographs
That lined her walls with comfort
And bring me to her other life –
A sepia land of country dachas, carriages
And wooden colonels taking tea.
We journeyed far from the damp, small flat,
With the ikons by the door, on the right,
The dust-woven rugs from Algeria
And the little, blackened blinis pan.

Baboushka, my life is fast and easy now;
I do not use your old and slow techniques,
But should it change as yours did
And leave me unprepared,
Please pray for me,
For I've lost my Bible and my wooden spoon.

Felicity Napier

Tropical Death

The fat black woman want
a brilliant tropical death
not a cold sojourn
in some North Europe far/forlorn

The fat black woman want
some heat/hibiscus at her feet
blue sea dress
to wrap her neat

The fat black woman want
some bawl
no quiet jerk tear wiping
a polite hearse withdrawal

The fat black woman want
all her dead rights
first night
third night
nine night
all the sleepless droning
red-eyed wake nights

In the heart
of her mother's sweetbreast
In the shade
of the sun leaf's cool bless
In the bloom
of her people's bloodrest

the fat black woman want
a brilliant tropical death yes

Grace Nichols

Elizabeth Gone

You lay in the nest of your real death,
Beyond the print of my nervous fingers
Where they touched your moving head;
Your old skin puckering, your lungs' breath
Grown baby short as you looked up last
At my face swinging over the human bed,
And somewhere you cried, *let me go let me go.*

You lay in the crate of your last death,
But were not you, not finally you.
They have stuffed her cheeks, I said;
This clay hand, this mask of Elizabeth
Are not true. From within the satin
And the suede of this inhuman bed,
Something cried, *let me go let me go.*

II

They gave me your ash and bony shells,
Rattling like gourds in the cardboard urn,
Rattling like stones that their oven had blest.
I waited you in the cathedral of spells
And I waited you in the country of the living,
Still with the urn crooned to my breast,
When something cried, *let me go let me go.*

So I threw out your last bony shells
And heard me scream for the look of you,
Your apple face, the simple crèche
Of your arms, the August smells
Of your skin. Then I sorted your clothes
And the loves you had left, Elizabeth,
Elizabeth, until you were gone.

Anne Sexton

Old Woman

So much she caused she cannot now account for
As she stands watching day return, the cool
Walls of the house moving towards the sun.
She puts some flowers in a vase and thinks
        'There is not much I can arrange
In here and now, but flowers are suppliant

As children never were. And love is now
A flicker of memory, my body is
My own entirely. When I lie at night
I gather nothing now into my arms,
        No child or man, and where I live
Is what remains when men and children go.'

Yet she owns more than residue of lives
That she has marked and altered. See how she
Warns time from too much touching her possessions
   By keeping flowers fed by polishing
        Her fine old silver. Gratefully
She sees her own glance printed on grandchildren.

Drawing the curtains back and opening windows
Every morning now, she feels her years
Grow less and less. Time puts no burden on
Her now she does not need to measure it.
        It is acceptance she arranges
And her own life she places in the vase.

                              Elizabeth Jennings

A woman undaunted

Mississippi Winter IV

My father and mother both
used to warn me
that 'a whistling woman and a crowing
hen would surely come to
no good end.' And perhaps I should
have listened to them.
But even at the time I knew
that though my end probably might
not
be good
I must whistle
like a woman undaunted
until I reached it.

Alice Walker

Taint

But I was stolen by men
the colour of my own skin
borne away by men whose heels
had become hoofs
whose hands had turned talons
bearing me down
    to the trail
of darkness

But I was traded by men
the colour of my own skin
traded like a fowl   like a goat
like a sack of kernels I was
traded
    for beads   for pans
for trinkets?

No it isn't easy to forget
what we refuse to remember

Daily I rinse the taint
of treachery from my mouth

                        Grace Nichols

Ala

Face up
they hold her naked body
to the ground
arms and legs spread-eagle
each tie with rope to stake

then they coat her in sweet
molasses and call us out
to see . . . . . the rebel woman

who with a pin
stick the soft mould
of her own child's head

sending the little-new-born
soul winging its way back
to Africa – free

they call us out to see
the fate for all us rebel
women

the slow and painful
picking away of the flesh
by red and pitiless ants

but while the ants feed
and the sun blind her with
his fury
we the women sing and weep
as we work

                    Grace Nichols

Holding My Beads

Unforgiving as the course of justice
Inerasable as my scars and fate
I am here
a woman . . . . . with all my lives
strung out like beads
                              before me
It isn't privilege or pity
that I seek
It isn't reverence or safety
quick happiness or purity
                              but
the power to be what I am/a woman
charting my own futures/   a woman
holding my beads in my hand

                    Grace Nichols

Lineage

My grandmothers were strong.
They followed plows and bent to toil.
They moved through fields sowing seed.
They touched earth and grain grew.
They were full of sturdiness and singing.
My grandmothers were strong.

My grandmothers are full of memories
Smelling of soap and onions and wet clay
With veins rolling roughly over quick hands
They have many clean words to say.
My grandmothers were strong.
Why am I not as they?

                                    Margaret Walker

An Even Shape

Her garden looks in through my window
Criss-crossed by the white lattice.
Coolers they call them but they are also
Hiding places for small girls playing.

Her garden stands neatly round her house
Travels politely unto the verandah
To sit in pots or hang
Leafily down from large, earth coloured urns.

She lives with Mama, shepherding with her full body
The hesitant ins and outs of Mama's half-blind days.
Feeding her frail consciousness with edited Gleaner
        news
And homemade chicken soup.

In her home, borrowed children touched her china
        birds with hands
Wiped clean from eating sticky cakes, each with a
        cherry on top
Or press moist, breathless kisses round
The corners of her smile.

Sometimes she fills the spaces out
With music. Spreading out nostalgia through
Strings and flutes, old fashioned love songs
Of blue moons and forever and until.

Shameful peeping Tom, I sit silent in
My lattice watching the even shape of her days
To catch, just once, a wider open door behind
Her steady eyes.

But in her green edged privacy, self-contained
She keeps the half-drawn shutters of her life
Open just so, and mocks my greed and restlessness
With a calm refusal to be other than she seems.

Christine Craig

get it & feel good

you cd just take what
he's got for you
i mean what's available
cd add up in the long run
if it's music/ take it
say he's got good
dishwashing techniques
he cd be a marvelous
masseur/ take it
whatever good there is to
get/ get it & feel good

say there's a electrical
wiring fanatic/ he cd
come in handy some day
suppose they know how to tend plants
if you want somebody
with guts/ you cd go to a rodeo
a prize fight/ or a gang war might be up your alley
there's somebody out there
with something you want/
not alla it/ but a lil
bit from here & there can
add up in the long run

whatever good there is to get
get it & feel good
this one's got kisses
that one can lay
linoleum

this one likes wine
that one fries butter fish
real good
this one is a anarcho-musicologist
this one wants pushkin to rise again
& that one has had it with the past tense/
whatever good there is to get/
get it & feel good
this one cd make music
roll around the small of
yr back & that one jumps
up & down in the gardens
it cd be yrs
there really is enuf to get
by with in this world but
you have to know what yr looking
for/ whatever good there is to get
get it & feel good
you have to know what
they will give up easily
what's available is not always
all that's possible
but there's so much fluctuation
in the market these days
you have to be
particular
whatever good there is to get
get it & feel good/ get it & feel good
snatch it & feel good
grab it & feel good
steal it & feel good
borrow it & feel good

reach it & feel good
you cd
    oh yeah
      & feel good.

Ntozake Shange

Notes to help your reading

No Dialects Please

7 *Dialects*: alternative forms of a language. The poet is refer-
ring to patois, a Caribbean form of English or French.
boushet: belly.

dialect of de Normans and de Saxons: This is the dialect of
English called 'Standard English' or 'proper English'
which has developed over centuries. Many of its features
are a result of invasions by the Saxons and the Normans.
It is a 'mongrel' language borrowing words and grammar
from many others.

language-elect: a supposedly superior form of English.

*de part of my story/dat come from Liverpool in a big dirty white
ship*: Ships set out from Liverpool and Bristol laden with
things to trade in Africa for slaves. The slaves were then
taken to the Caribbean and the Americas and sold.

plantations: estates on which cotton or tobacco are culti-
vated and harvested by slave labour

8 *Butler*: a powerful pro-British trade unionist in Trinidad.
He helped organise strikes in the oil industry. He was
arrested and detained through the war because the Amer-
icans needed the oil and feared he would stop its production.

dunce: stupid (dialect).

oui: Yes. Some dialects or patois use French. This was the
main European language spoken in certain Caribbean
islands.

Stillborn

11 *pickling fluid*: a liquid to preserve things that would other-

wise rot. A human embryo can be stored in a glass jar full of this fluid. Sometimes you can see them in museums. This is what she is referring to.

It must

15 *pigment*: skin coloration.
   raddled: literally rouged, but meaning aged and garish.
16 *taboo words*: words we are not allowed to say.
   frost-touched fruit: If fruits are touched by frost they rot.

House of Changes

17 *commune*: a house where a number of people live together sharing all costs and responsibilities.
   perceptions: what she notices about people.
18 *Commendable*: worthy of praise.
   Equivocal: undecided.
19 *Imminent*: about to happen.

The Woman in the Ordinary

20 *effaces*: makes invisible.
   golden fleece: Jason and the argonauts sought the fabulous golden fleece, so Greek mythology tells us. Golden Fleece now represents anything wonderful and hard to obtain.
   yam: a tropical vegetable.
   goldenrod: dramatic and beautiful flower.

Ye housewyf

22 The fun of this poem is in guessing the meanings. It is

written in a comic version of the English of Chaucer's times, the fourteenth century. Some words are no longer used in modern English and I offer the translation from Middle English.

coverchief: scarf.

Fetis: neat.

eek: also.

Hänged: hung.

carp: talk.

To Friends

22 *grappling hooks*: used by mountaineers to secure their ropes.

Love Should Grow Up Like a Wild Iris in the Fields

25 *sidewalk*: pavement (American).

iris of any eye: the coloured part of the eye surrounding the pupil.

Even Tho

26 *star-apple*: a soft sweet fruit.

sea moss: soft seaweed.

night letter

29 *swami*: Hindu religious teacher.

30 *collect calls*: phone calls when the person who answers the phone pays the cost.

Rondeau Redoublé

35 *Rondeau*: a poem using repetition.
Redoublé: re-echoed: the idea goes round and round.
Zen: a form of the Buddhist religion which stresses looking inside yourself to understand life and death.
cryptic homilies: mystical sermons making little sense.
Tony Benn: a passionate socialist.
yen: Japanese currency.

Blue Moles

40 *orbit*: a circular route.
carcass: dead body.
veteran: old soldier.
pelt: skin.
Palming: shoving with the palms of their 'hands'.
grubbers: diggers, rummagers.
41 *appendages*: loose bits.
sweetbreads: internal pancreas, but meaning tasty morsels.
shards: beetles' wing covers.
surfeit: over-indulgence – eating too much.

Not Waving but Drowning

42 *larking*: playing foolishly.

Child

43 *meditate*: think about.
troublous: agitated, distressed.

Lost, Never Found

46 *Arcturus*: a star.

'*Marie Celeste*': a ship from which the entire crew mysteriously disappeared.

kayaks: Eskimo canoes.

junks: Chinese flat-bottomed boats.

triremes: Greek warships with three banks of oars.

47 *forwarding address*: address at which they may be contacted.

double-audited (accounts): double-checked.

Thebes or Alexandria or Rome: capital cities and centres of ancient civilisations.

48 *Romanov*: Royal family in Russia before the 1917 Revolution.

Limoges: an area in France famous for fine pottery.

Sarajevo: town in Yugoslavia where Archduke Ferdinand was assassinated in 1914. This event led to the start of the First World War.

Croat: Eastern European language.

Somme: an area of France where thousands of soldiers were killed in the First World War.

Hiroshima, 1945

50 *Hiroshima*: A city in Japan on which the Americans dropped the first atom bomb, causing terrible devastation and long-term damage.

sun slips: The nuclear explosion blots out the sun.

It is only eight fifteen: Although it is early morning the sun has vanished.

shadow on the step: The heat and glare of the explosion is so powerful that people caught in it are dissolved. Their burning bodies scorch the ground leaving eerie shadow shapes wherever they fall.

The Fifth Sense

52 *coil in the red/Scent of the fox*: smell the traces of the fox in the wood.

53 *They would fire at a rainbow*: The soldiers are trained to do exactly what they are told and to destroy anything which doesn't match what they are taught.

Charivari

56 *Charivari*: a ritual to humiliate an unpopular person, serenading him or her with the noise of banging pans or, as here, broken instruments.

the white bride: The charivari is held to show disapproval of the black man marrying a white woman.

Victims

57 *exile*: The poem is about refugees who have left their country to escape persecution or death.

spastic: someone suffering from brain damage causing involuntary muscle movement.

straitjacket: a primitive way of controlling demented people by restricting their movement. The jacket stops their arms from moving at all. Normal life is like a straitjacket for this boy so damaged by his experiences.

58 *niche*: comfortable, appropriate place.

icon: a sacred image.

memento mori: reminder that death comes to us all.

the place of burning: Adolf Hitler tried to exterminate all Jews. They were taken to concentration camps where many millions were gassed in specially built gas chambers. Millions more died of starvation and neglect. Their bodies were burned or buried in vast pits.

Absit omen: a Latin phrase: may what I fear not come true.

graffito: a sign for all to read.

coat of ash seared in: their experience has burnt into them a sense of the horrors of death and destruction.

delicate cloak of fat: they know no such thing – they are easily burnt, easily hurt.

The Anti-suffragists

59 *suffragists*: women fighting for equal rights for women.

deference: putting them first.

naught: nothing.

renounce: give up.

principles of righteous government: the underlying idea of equality and justice.

60 *those before*: Other women had to fight for these women to have their education.

sublimely: extraordinarily, blissfully.

aspiration: hope.

conscientious women: women with a conscience – who want to do good things.

old king: Canute, who ordered the sea to go back.

I Am a Union Woman

62 *NMU*: National Miners' Union.

Rooshian Red: Russian Communist.

With Child

66 *languid*: slow-moving.

Torpid: slow, lazy.

You cleft me with your beauty's pulse: His beauty was warm and pulsing. It was like an instrument hammering at wood until it splits. She could not resist and opened her heart and body to him.

Your pulse has taken body: This pulse is the rhythm of orgasm. It 'has taken body' – she has become pregnant.

little death: The Elizabethans called sex 'the little death' thinking that every time a man ejaculated sperm, he died a little, while the sperm went on to make new life.

stark: bare, unwelcoming.

tugs and moans: from about twenty weeks a mother feels the very clear and increasingly strong movements of her unborn baby.

For a Child Expected

67   *secret setting of a child*: to make a baby.

    candle immortal: They think they are making their love immortal – that it will live forever in their child.

    Its life is the body of his love: The baby is brought into existence by his love.

67   *like his caress,/First delicate and strange, that daily use/Makes dearer and priceless*: The mother's awareness that she is carrying a live baby inside her is at first as strange and tender as her first lovemaking. When daily use gets her accustomed to lovemaking, it feels dearer and priceless. So with the baby's movements, as she gets used to them, they feel all the more beautiful.

    painter's ... coiled hearing: They wanted the child to have the skills and joys of painters and poets.

    The world flowed in: They wanted for the child everything that is beautiful in the world.

68   *Cat's cradle of hopes*: A cat's cradle is a complicated pattern of string. This net of hopes was not strong enough to tie a baby in. She brings her own hopes and joys and fears with her: 'what we began/Is now its own'.

    Unperturbed: undisturbed.

The Abortion

69 *Rumpelstiltskin*: a fairy-tale character, a small man who, in return for favours to the Queen, claimed her child. She could only get the child back if she guessed his name correctly.

For a Child Born Dead

71 *mould*: shape.

Poem to My Daughter

72 *corpulent*: very fat.
deliver: The midwife claims that she does all the work!
hostage to fortune: something that you acquire which you love dearly and which, if lost, would cause you terrible pain.
bloodcord: the umbilical cord through which the baby has been fed.

Transformation

73 *phoenix*: a legendary bird supposed to rise again from its own ashes.
placenta: the organ which has fed the baby. Also called the afterbirth, it is delivered a few minutes after the baby.
74 *stitch*: Women are often cut to ease the birth and sewn up again afterwards. A local anaesthetic is used and the stitching does not hurt. It can take quite some time.
translucent: allowing light to shine through.

Dawn

75 *agate*: a semi-precious stone.

Emperor Baby

78 *Gossed*: This is the poet's own word. We are to guess at the meaning. Two possibilities are (a) as if covered in gossamer or fine down; (b) looking like gossan, a quartz-type rock containing iron compounds. The threads of metallic substance in the rock could look like the baby's hair.

marble breast: Her breasts, full of milk, have prominent veins like those which give marble its pattern.

drunken: with joy.

Heirloom

82 *Heirloom*: a precious thing passed on from generation to generation.

Eyebright: a plant formerly used to treat diseases of the eye.

tormentil: low herb with bright yellow flowers.

lichen: plant growing on rocks, trees, walls.

corbies: ravens.

rowan: a small tree.

burn: stream.

Medusa: jellyfish.

Cowries: shells.

skein: a bundle of wool. Made by coiling it many times.

Mama

83 *tie-and-dye maxi*: a long dress or skirt coloured with a tie-

and-dye technique which creates a random pattern, very fashionable in the late 1960s.

sneakers: casual shoes like plimsolls.

Corona Smith: a brand of typewriter.

84 *okro*: a green vegetable which becomes slippery when cooked.

Pain for a Daughter

86 *distemper*: a disease causing fever and breathing disorder.

hydrogen peroxide: a powerful disinfectant.

not zoned for barns: area where you are not allowed to build barns.

burn like a furnace: perform like a powerful strong horse.

seat: bottom.

Skins

93 *cuticles*: cast-off skins.

crazes: makes random patterns on – i.e. the wrinkles in her skin.

incarnations: An incarnation means 'being made flesh', being born into a body. She has shed many bodies, many skins, since she was thirty. The poems, like the incarnations, have dropped off, and no longer have anything to do with her.

Blinis

94 *Blinis*: Russian raised pancakes

sepia: the brown and beige of photos taken in the early years of this century.

dachas: country residences of Russian gentlefolk and aristocrats.

ikons: holy pictures.

Tropical Death

96 *hibiscus*: vivid tropical flower.

97 *hearse*: the car which contains the coffin.

Elizabeth Gone

98 *gourds*: a fruit which rattles when dry.

urn: a container for ashes of a cremated person.

99 *crèche*: a place where children are cared for.

Old Woman

100 *suppliant*: humble, prepared to do what she asks.

Mississippi Winter IV

102 *undaunted*: not put off by anything.

Taint

103 *Taint*: to make dirty, the sense of feeling soiled.

the colour of my own skin: African slaves were often taken into captivity by black men paid by whites for their captives.

Ala

104 *molasses*: sugary syrup.
 stick the soft mould: She killed her baby by sticking a pin into the gap in its skull (the fontanelle) which all babies have. The skull is soft and flexible because it has to be squeezed through the birth canal. These gaps fill in in time.
 free: There are documented examples of slaves doing this, killing their babies to save them from an intolerable life of slavery.
 picking away of the flesh: The ants are attracted by the molasses and start to eat that and then her.

Holding My Beads

105 *Inerasable*: unable to be rubbed out.

Lineage

106 *Lineage*: a line of descent, mother to daughter and so on.

An Even Shape

107 *lattice*: a criss-cross pattern on a window.
 frail consciousness: She is only just aware of things and isn't to be shocked by any sensational news.
 Gleaner: a Jamaican newspaper.
 nostalgia: sentimental memory of happy days long past.
108 *self-contained*: content to stay in the boundaries of her own life – not needing to include others.

get it & feel good

109 *masseur*: a person skilled in massage.

rodeo: where men demonstrate horse-riding skills, often on horses no one else can ride.

prize fight: boxing match.

110 *anarcho-musicologist*: a student of music who does not believe in formal structures. This is a bit difficult as music relies on structures.

pushkin: a great Russian writer killed in a duel defending his wife's honour.

had it with the past tense: only who lives in the present. The only thing that matters is today.

fluctuation/in the market: change in the value of things.

Now you have read the poems

What follows is a range of coursework assignments for GCSE including:

    oral assignments

    personal response

    critical response

    your own writing.

They are arranged in three main parts:

    A Section by section

    B The whole anthology

    C Wider reading.

Keeping a reading log

As you begin to work through the anthology, you will find that you will need to take notes, jot down ideas and draft poems of your own.

You will need to keep your own reading log to store all this material which you can refer to for coursework assignments. For simplicity of organisation, it would be best to divide your log into sections just as the anthology is divided. Within each section of your log you will need the following subsections:

    Notes on poems generally

    Images

    Structures

    Essay plans

    Drafts of your own poems.

Building up your own poetry anthology

Many of the study assignments involve you in writing poems. It's very rare to find that you can write an excellent poem on your first attempt. You need to draft and redraft, looking at how to get each word to work to the very best effect. Look at
– images: are they clear?
                                    original?
                                    striking?
– sound patterns: do they work?
– line lengths: do they lead the reader through the poem?

    When you feel that you are happy with a poem, write it into your own anthology. These poems can be submitted as GCSE coursework.

Coursework assignments: section by section

The poems have been grouped into smaller units so that you can explore what they have in common and so that ideas from one poem will add to those from another. There are nine sections in all.

Oral assignments

These general assignments may be used with each section in turn. There is a range of suggestions. Some assignments simply help you find your way into the section or the poems. Some will help you build up notes and reflections to help with the later written tasks. Others are more demanding and can be used as specific GCSE oral tasks. They are marked with an asterisk*.

You will need to work in pairs and in small groups. It will help if you stay with the same group for all the tasks because you will learn to work together.

You will need to develop the following group skills:
– Try to listen sensitively.
– Give everyone's ideas a fair hearing.
– Don't let others do the work for you.
– Work together to focus on the task.
– Share your ideas generously.
– Don't be shy in offering ideas – there are no right and wrong answers. Your insight will help others.
– Together plan how you will jot down notes of your discussion for later use – one secretary? everyone taking notes?
– Ask one person to lead the discussion and take turns in this important task – it's a very useful skill to learn.
– Always take a few moments at the end to review what you

have discussed and to check that you have got the notes complete.

Assignments

1 When you have read each section discuss the poems. Here are some ideas to help you organise the discussion. Take brief notes of your discussion, these will help with later coursework tasks.
   - What is the section about? Jot down a few words which will sum up its theme.
   - Which poems did you like straight away? Why?
   - Which poems are you still puzzling over? Read them together and discuss them. Look at the section 'Before you start reading' (page xii) for some ideas on how to read poems.

2 Choose one or two of the poems to read aloud. You may need to work in pairs for this as some of the poems need two voices. Concentrate on the sound pattern the poet has designed and make sure that your reading lets the pattern shine through.

3 *You could extend the reading into a talk lasting at least five minutes. Again choose one or two poems that you enjoy. Practise reading them so that a listener will understand and enjoy them. Try them out in your group and take advice from your friends.

   Add to the reading some of your own thoughts about the poem(s) such as:
   - explaining why you chose it/them
   - explaining the images the poet uses
   - talking about the sound pattern she has created
   - comparing it to other poems in the section which have similar themes or images.

   You will need to make notes about all these things and anything else you want to say. It may help you to write it

129

all out as an essay. This could be used as piece of written coursework. When it comes to giving the talk though, you must not just read out the essay – that would be dull and flat. It's best to make brief notes that you can glance down at from time to time.

4 Many of the poems are dramatic. You can easily turn them into a play with one or more characters. Try doing an improvisation around one or more poems and discuss what happens when you no longer have the poets' language to enrich the story or the characters.

5 *This too could develop into an assignment piece if you planned it carefully and developed the characters and the story fully and followed it by a reading of the poem which sparked the idea.

Section 1: I'm in here hiding from words

Personal response

Assignment 1

The poems are about the difficulty and the joy of writing poetry. You will have been asked to write poems, stories and essays many times. Think about how you have reacted when you have tried to write for a teacher or for yourself.

Use these thoughts as the basis for
– *a piece of writing. You could perhaps call it 'Me and a blank sheet of paper'.*
– *a poem of your own which could fit in this section.*

– a discussion within your group about problems you have in writing and how you deal with them. Share any good ideas with the rest of the class.

Assignment 2: 'No Dialects Please'

Look at the section 'Notes to help your reading' (page 112) if you have difficulty with this poem.

Many of the poems and all of the editorial material (parts written by the editor) are written in a dialect or form of English called Standard English, sometimes called 'proper' English. Many of us also can use other dialects of English that are shared with the people in the area where we live, such as the Cockney dialect used by Londoners, or the Geordie dialect used by people from Newcastle. A dialect has three main features:

– pronunciation: You can often tell where people come from because of their accent.
– special words: Some words are only used in certain parts of the country, for example the word 'mardy' meaning bad-tempered or sulky is mostly used in the north of England.
– grammar: Here is an example from the poem of the grammar used in this Caribbean dialect; 'To tink how still dey so dunce' meaning 'To think how they are still so dunce (stupid)'. It differs from the grammar of Standard English.

Read the poem out loud and let the poet's spelling guide your pronunciation.

Discuss what Merle Collins is saying. Note the main points she is making. Use them in a letter to the organiser of the poetry competition. Write one version in Standard English and one in your own local dialect if you have one.

Assignment 3: 'Silence is Nearer to Truth'

Did this ring a bell? Has a teacher ever put you down like this? Discuss your experience or imagine how it must feel.

131

Write a letter in which you tell the teacher how she failed you and how you felt.

Think of it from her point of view. Is it possible to be sensitive, caring and encouraging all day, every day? Write a teacher's diary for a week and include in it her worries about accidentally discouraging someone. You will need to research her experience of work to do this well.

Critical response

Assignment 4: looking at images

For this section, it will be enough to make notes of how the poets use images to develop an idea or share an emotion. Keep these notes in your reading log to use in later assignments.

(a) Start with 'Stillborn' by Sylvia Plath (page 11). Below are some discussion points to help you. Note down your findings in your reading log.

Look at verse 1. What does she mean by 'These poems do not live'? Why does she compare them to babies? What does she mean by 'It wasn't for any lack of mother-love'?

Look at verse 2. 'They sit so nicely in the pickling fluid!' Sylvia Plath is referring to a way of preserving dead human fetuses for study by putting them in special fluid in a glass jar or container so they can be seen. Often exhibits, like lambs with five legs, are kept like this and shown in museums or fairgrounds.

Why does she use this image to describe her poems?

Look at verse 3. Why do the poems 'have a piggy and a fishy air'? (An 'air' can mean a likeness or a smell.)

What does she mean by

But they are dead, and their mother near dead with distraction

And they stupidly stare, and do not speak of her?

The whole poem is one extended *metaphor*. Sylvia Plath has transformed the poems she doesn't like into stillborn babies – they die before they are even born. This idea goes right the way through the poem.

It is very clever because these bad poems are like stillborn babies in lots of ways:
– both are created by the poet.
– both need lots of small pieces to function for them to live happily. Poems need words and images, babies need fingers, toes, brains: 'Their little foreheads bulged with concentration'.
– both need mother love.
– both need something special to make them live – a heart beat, the rise and fall of the lungs, the rhythm of the poem.
– if they are 'alive' and functioning well they 'speak of' their mother. They offer an image of her.

(b) Now go on to study metaphor in 'I'm In Here Hiding' by Lorna Goodison (page 4). Again make notes in your reading log in the section you have labelled Images.

Here are some questions to help focus your discussion.
– Follow the idea of birds through the poem. What do the birds do?
– What do words do to Lorna Goodison and why does she want to hide from them?
– How can she shut doors and windows against them?
– Why does she talk about 'high pains of windows'?

Keep these notes; you will add to them later and you will need them for some of the later assignments.

Assignment 5: looking at structure

In this section you will produce a short description of the structure of a poem and learn how to quote from poems.

(a) Start with Alice Walker's poem: 'How Poems Are Made/A Discredited View'. Read it silently first and then out loud. In your reading notice the verses and the repetition.

Discuss the structure and make notes about the way Alice has organised the poem.

Here are questions to help.

Letting go
in order to hold on
I gradually understand
how poems are made.

> Why are these two ideas on different lines?
> Why does she have this very short opening verse?
> Why is it separate from the next verse?

There is a place the fear must go.
There is a place the choice must go.
There is a place the loss must go.
The leftover love.

> Why does she repeat the line structure?

The love that spills out
of the too full cup
and runs and hides
its too full self
in shame.

> What effect does she get by letting these lines run into each other?

I gradually comprehend
how poems are made.
To the upbeat flight of memories.
The flagged beats of the running heart.

> Why the break?
> Why does she echo verse one?

I understand how poems are made.
They are the tears
that season the smile.
The stiff-neck laughter
that crowds the throat.
The leftover love.

> What echoes are made here?

I know how poems are made.

There is a place the loss must
   go.
There is a place the gain must
   go.
The leftover love.

How does she bring it all together?

Now look again at 'Stillborn'. (Read it quietly and then out loud.) What patterns can you see in Sylvia Plath's poem? Look at

– rhymes
– number of lines in each verse
– repetition
– the length of lines – why are some longer than others?
– the last line of each verse. Is it more important than the others?

What is the effect of all these patterns on the poem? Do you enjoy them as you read the poem?

(b) Make brief notes to help you with the next task.

(c) Now write a short piece on how the structure of these two poems helps the poet share her ideas and emotions with us.

Before you start, discuss the main points you want to make and jot them down. A good way of doing this is in a topic web like this:

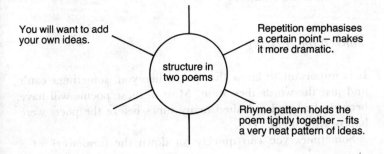

You will want to add your own ideas.

Repetition emphasises a certain point – makes it more dramatic.

structure in two poems

Rhyme pattern holds the poem tightly together – fits a very neat pattern of ideas.

135

Go through the poems looking for examples of each point you want to make.

You will want to quote certain lines to demonstrate a point. For example, you might want to talk about Sylvia Plath's use of repetition. This is how you would do it.

Sylvia Plath uses a striking image to convey her frustration at her unsatisfactory poems. She compares them to stillborn babies. She extends the comparison to liken them to fetuses on display in glass jars. Here she uses repetition to push home the powerful effect of the metaphor:

'They smile and smile and smile and smile at me.'

– Use colons to indicate you are about to quote.
– Use quote marks to indicate start and finish of quote.
– Lay out the quote so it is clear and separate from your writing.
– Keep the poet's line structure.

You might just want to quote the odd word or phrase. In that case you set it out like this:

Sylvia Plath shocks us with her image of the stillborn poems with their 'piggy and (a) fishy air' of rotting ideas.

– Put the words or phrases from the poem in quotes.
– If you don't want to use a particular word, just put it in brackets.

Use this writing exercise to practise using quotes and explaining structure. Keep the piece you produce, you will be able to refer to it later.

Your own writing

It is important to know that poets, like you, sometimes can't find just the words they want. Most of these poems will have been drafted and redrafted many times before the poets were happy with them.

Sometimes you can quickly jot down the framework of a

poem, but then it needs working as a skilled woodworker makes a carving. You need to develop images, decide on structures, tune it so that its sound echoes your meaning.

Many ideas and experiences can trigger poems. Here are some based on this section which might serve as starting points.

Dialect poems

Poems written in a local dialect often have great directness and energy. Look at how well 'No Dialects Please' shows Merle Collins' amused anger. There are several dialect poems in this anthology; look at these poems by Ntozake Shange:

'night letter', pages 28–30
'lady in blue', pages 31–2
'get it & feel good', pages 109–11

written in a black American dialect, and these poems by Grace Nichols:

'We the Women', page 14
'Even Tho', pages 26–7
'Tropical Death', page 96–7

written in a West Indian dialect.

If you use a local dialect as well as Standard English, you could try writing in that dialect. Use the tricks these poets use of letting the spelling of the word show the reader how to pronounce it.

If you don't use a local dialect yourself, you could still try a dialect poem and ask someone who uses the dialect to advise you.

What are poems about? Where do they come from?

Alice Walker thinks she knows:

137

> There is a place the loss must go.
> There is a place the gain must go.
> The leftover love.

And that place is a poem. What goes into your poem?
Write a sister poem to Alice Walker's saying where your poems
come from.

Try to use some of the structures you have looked at here
in your own poems: repetition, verses, rhymes and line
lengths.

Section 2: We the women

Personal response

Assignment 6: 'We the Women'

Are women undervalued as Grace Nichols suggests?

> Yet we the women
> who praises go unsung
> who voices go unheard
> who deaths they sweep
> aside
> as easy as dead leaves

Look at this poem and 'Three Poems for Women' (page 21).
What are the poets saying and do you agree? Discuss the
poems and what they say about women's roles.

*Plan and write an essay with this title: 'The praises of women go
unsung, their voices go unheard'. Do you agree?*

Start by brainstorming – collecting together as many ideas as
possible as quickly as possible. It's a good idea to note them
down on a topic web like this one which just explores one or
two ideas:

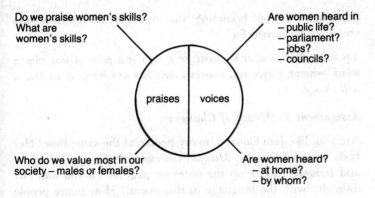

Do we praise women's skills?
What are
women's skills?

Are women heard in
– public life?
– parliament?
– jobs?
– councils?

praises   voices

Who do we value most in our
society – males or females?

Are women heard?
– at home?
– by whom?

– At this point you may need to go to the library and research some facts and figures.

– When you've roughly collected your ideas, start to organise them into a plan – work out which order you will put them in.

– Think very hard about your opening paragraph. Use it to introduce your reader to the essay and to prepare her or him for what you are going to say.

– Work your way through the points you want to make.

– Make sure you show that you have thought about other points of view.

– Use your last paragraph to draw the essay to an end and summarise your main points.

Assignment 7: 'It Must'

What do you think when you look, really look, into the mirror? What will your face look like as you age? What will it tell about you? Ruth Fainlight says she isn't always depressed by the signs of ageing. She asks:

> Do you also
> sometimes feel a sudden jaunty indifference,
> or even better, extraordinary moments
> when you positively welcome the new
> face that greets you from the mirror

139

She can see herself becoming 'that other/dream-figure of she-you-always-yearned-for'.

Try using these ideas as the basis for a story or a poem of your own in which someone, maybe you, examines their face and begins to see how it will change.

Assignment 8: 'House of Changes'

Are you, like Jeni Couzyn, many people at the same time? Her body houses *Vulnerable, Mindful, Commendable, Equivocal, Harmful* and *Imminent*. (Look up the notes on page 113 if you find any difficulty with the language in this poem.) How many people live in your body? Are they all nice, gentle people? Are there some you don't like?

Explore this idea in a poem, a story or even a play where they meet and possibly disagree.

Start by reading the poem very carefully and noticing how Jeni Couzyn has developed the personality of each of her personae (people she has made up).

You should also read 'The Woman in the Ordinary' (page 20), which is similar. Here a powerful woman hides within an 'ordinary pudgy downcast girl'. It makes you look for hidden strength in all women.

Assignment 9: 'Ye Housewyf'

Look at the notes on page 113 if you have any difficulty with this poem. It is a parody (a literary 'take-off') of Chaucer and is written in 'mock' fourteenth-century English. You will look at how it works in the Critical Response section.

For now, look at its theme and compare it with 'Three Poems for Women' (page 21). 'The Housewyf' is a jaunty woman even though she 'loved the sink the least in all the lands'.

The women in Susan Griffin's poem are quite different. Read the three sections and discuss why they neither hear nor speak. Susan Griffin invites you to

140

Stare at an empty space and imagine her there,
the woman with children
because she cannot be here to speak
for herself,
and listen
to what you think
she might say.

Discuss what she and 'the housewyf' might say about their lives. Think carefully about the language they would use. Present your ideas as a poem, a short play or a radio interview.

Assignment 10: 'To Friends'

Read the poem and discuss Anna Dolezal's metaphor. Does it ring true for you? How would you explain the help and joy that friends give you? Do you think that friendship between women is different from that between women and men and from that between men and men?

(a) Use these questions as the starting point for a small group and, if possible, a whole class discussion.

During the discussion, note whether males and females disagree about kinds of friendship. Does any one tend to 'put down' women's friendships as being all 'girl-talk' and gossip? What do men and boys talk about?

(b) You can use the discussion to help you plan an essay or a poem on friendship.

Critical response

Assignment 11: looking at structures

The two long poems in this section, 'It Must' and 'House of Changes', are organised in verses which work like paragraphs in essays.

Look carefully at the two poems and discuss the following questions.

– What is each verse about? Note down its main idea in a few words.
– Follow the development of each verse – what does it add to what has gone before?
– Look carefully at the first and last verse – how do they differ from the others?

Make notes in your reading log of your discussion.

Think about the way these poems are organised when you set about writing longer poems yourself or when you are writing essays.

Assignment 12: looking at images

Read 'House of Changes' (page 17) carefully and think about the images Jeni Couzyn presents. Make notes as you go along. The whole poem is one extended metaphor in which the poet is 'transformed' into a house containing several different women; Vulnerable, Mindful, Commendable, Equivocal and Harmful. At the same time she is another character: Imminent, 'making friends with them all/unobtrusively, slow and steady/slow and steady'.

This particular kind of imagery is called *allegory*. Its features are:
– an extended metaphor
– abstract qualities like worthiness, vulnerability are *personified*.
In other words, they are made into personae or dramatic characters – Vulnerable, Commendable, etc.

There are three very famous examples of allegorical writing: *Everyman* (Anon), *Pilgrim's Progress* by John Bunyan and *The Faerie Queen* by Edmund Spenser. All of them should be in your library. *The Faerie Queen* is the most recent and it was published in 1596! Although examples of allegorical writing do occur right up to the present day it has been used less and less. It is actually a very useful device if you want to divide a person up into her different qualities and have each part performing and sometimes conflicting.

(a) Try the technique yourself. If your poem shows understanding of the technique then it should be an acceptable piece of coursework in this section.

This is how to set about it:

– Read 'House of Changes' again and discuss how much you learn about the woman in the poem.

– If you can do so, read at least part of *Everyman* or *Pilgrim's Progress*. You could try *The Faerie Queen* too but that is quite complex so the other two are better starting points.

– Think about the content of your poem. Are you going to describe a person or an experience? Here are some qualities or concepts which could be transformed into personae for your allegorical poem. You can add many ideas of your own.

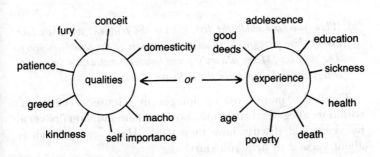

– You can see how the *qualities* might be transformed by the *experiences*. What would happen if Self Importance or Conceit met Education? Perhaps Self Importance would learn there's more to life than putting herself first!

– Once you have worked out your characters, put them in some kind of context. Are they on a journey? Are they past, present or future characters? What kind of world do they inhabit?

- Now start trying to find a suitable structure to fit what you have to say: verses? rhhymes? rhythm?
- Do a first draft. Discuss it with your group. Try again and again, until you have got it right.

Now read 'The Woman in the Ordinary'. This poem is structured around images which contrast violently with each other. They demonstrate that within each ordinary woman is someone uproarious, high-spirited, noisy. Someone you have to notice. Look at the poem carefully and note the contrasts in your log under these headings. The first few are done for you.

Ordinary	Uproarious
pudgy	massive thighs
downcast	neigh
crouching	
round	

(b) *When you have made the list, discuss the contrasts and then take two or three paragraphs to write an analysis of the poem's imagery. The title is: 'Marge Piercy's poem balances contrasting images to convey the real woman in the ordinary – discuss.'*

There are many striking images in 'House of Changes' within its allegorical structure. Look at them individually verse by verse and discuss how they work. Here are some ideas about verse 2 to help you start.

Nearest the door	Why is she nearest the door?
ready in her black leather	
is *Vulnerable*. She lives in the hall	
her face painted with care	What does this mean?
her black boots reaching her crotch	Why is she dressed like this?
her black hair shining	
her skin milky and soft as butter.	Why the contrast?

144

If you should ring the doorbell
she would answer
and a wound would open across   Why?
   her eyes
as she touched your hand.

(c) Now that you have practised writing shorter pieces of analysis, you can move on to a full-length essay on this poem. Use the ideas and notes you have from the other assignments on the poem. The title is: '"House of Changes" – a critical analysis.'

Look at the following:
– content and meaning
– structure
– imagery: the allegorical structure and the images throughout
   the poem
– sound patterns: repetitions, rhythms and line lengths.

Compare it with other poems in this section or in the anthology if you think that would help you explain or elaborate a point.

Assignment 13: looking at styles

'Ye Housewyf' is a parody. That means it is a comic take-off, a mimicry of Chaucer's language style and content. The Housewyf could almost be one of the characters in Chaucer's *Canterbury Tales*. Here is his Wife of Bath:

Hir coverchiefs ful fyne weren of ground
I dorste swere they weyeden ten pound
That on a Sonday weren upon hir heed.
Hir hosen weren of fyn scarlet reed
Ful streite yteyd and shoes ful moyste and newe.
Boold was hir face, and fair, and reed of hewe.
She was a worthy womman al hir lyve
Housebondes at chirch dore she hadde fyve,
Withouten oother compaignye in youthe . . .
Gat tothed was she, soothly for to seye

145

Upon an amblere esily she sat,
Ywympled wel, and on hir heed an hat
As brood as is a bokeler or a targe;
A foot-mantel aboute hir hipes large,
And on hir feet a paire of spores sharpe.
In felaweshipe wel koude she laughe and carpe.
Of remedies of love she knew perchaunce,
For she koude of that art the old dance.

And here is Neville Coghill's translation of those lines:

Her kerchiefs were of finely woven ground;
I dared have sworn they weighed a good ten pound,
The ones she wore on Sunday, on her head.
Her hose were of the finest scarlet red
And gartered tight; her shoes were soft and new.
Bold was her face, handsome, and red in hue.
A worthy woman all her life, what's more
She'd had five husbands, all at the church door,
Apart from other company in youth . . .
She had gap-teeth, set widely, truth to say.
Easily on an ambling horse she sat
Well wimpled up, and on her head a hat
As broad as is a buckler or a shield;
She had a flowing mantle that concealed
Large hips, her heels spurred sharply under that.
In company she liked to laugh and chat
And knew the remedies for love's mischances.
An art in which she knew the oldest dances.

(a) *Discuss the original and the parody and note down all parallels you can find between the two.*

Meg Wanless assumes that her reader will recognise that she is parodying Chaucer and this is part of the fun of the poem. She also enjoys making up fake fourteenth-century English. Many words and phrases refer to things which simply would not have existed in the Middle Ages.

(b) Look carefully at the poem and find as many examples of this fake language as you can.

(c) Try a parody of your own. Again this can count as coursework if your parody shows clearly how well you have analysed and understood the poem you are copying. Choose one of the poems in this anthology and write 'in the style of' the poet.

Here are some suggestions of ones worth considering; 'Still-born' (page 11), 'Three Poems for Women' (page 21), 'Ye Housewyf' (page 22), 'Even Tho' (page 26), 'night letter' (page 28), 'I Am Union Woman' (page 62), 'Transformation' (page 73) and 'Tropical Death' (page 96).

Section 3: Like a wild iris in the fields

Personal response

Assignment 14: 'Love Should Grow Up Like a Wild Iris in the Fields'

Read the poem carefully and discuss what Susan Griffin is saying about love. Use these headings to make notes about love:

love should be	love really is
like a wild iris growing after a storm	the way people feel 'in kitchens at the dinner hour', 'tired out and hungry'

Now try to make your own set of notes. Here are one or two ideas to get you started. Look at the other poems in this section to give you more ideas.

147

How I think love should be	What it's really like to feel loved and to give love
dancing together in the moonlight	how you feel when you suddenly think someone you love might die.
gazing into your loved one's eyes	finding a way of putting up with his annoying little ways.

Now use your notes to help you try your own version of Susan Griffin's poem. Contrast your romantic ideal with a much more down-to-earth description of love.

Assignment 15: 'night letter'

In this poem Ntozake Shange writes an imaginary letter to

old lovers i never want to see
  lovers i'm dying to meet

We see her confusion, her sadness, her hope, leaving her

    on the wharf
  callin sea gulls

trying to communicate to people who cannot hear her.

Read the poem out loud. It would be helpful to do this in pairs using different voices for different parts.

Now try writing your own night letter in prose or poetry to people (real or imaginary) who don't hear you, don't understand what you have to say. Tell them what you feel and think.

Assignment 16: 'lady in blue'

Have you ever wanted to tell someone exactly what you thought of them and not been able to find the words at the right time?

148

Remember or imagine a time when someone you love has been unkind or heartless and try to say exactly how angry you are. Use Ntozake Shange's opening lines for your title:

> one thing i dont need
> is any more apologies

Look carefully at the poem and see how she shows her anger. You can use prose or poetry to express yours.

Assignment 17: 'Dawn Walkers'

Read the poem carefully and think about the scene Jenny Joseph describes. In your group discuss what has happened. Imagine the scene before John left – what might have occurred? Use these ideas as the basis for a drama improvisation. Accompany it with a reading of the poem. This could be an oral assignment for GCSE.

Assignment 18: 'Rondeau Redoublé'

(a) Imagine you are the woman in this poem and have made all her mistakes. Write to the agony column of a woman's magazine explaining about your disastrous love life. Then change personalities and write the agony aunt's reply. Try to give concise, helpful advice.

(b) Now use the same material for a drama improvisation in pairs. One person should be the woman who makes mistakes and the other her long-suffering friend giving advice. Accompany the improvisation with a reading of the poem.

Critical response

Assignment 19: looking at style

'night letter' and 'lady in blue' by Ntozake Shange both use a similar style. If you look at the very last poem in the anthology, 'get it & feel good', also by the same poet, you will notice many similarities.

(a) Read all three out loud and discuss what they have in common. Here are some statements about the style of the poems. Which do you think are true? Jot down some notes in your reading log giving reasons for your answers and quotes from the poems to support them.

True or false?
Ntozake Shange is a British poet.
She uses old-fashioned language.
The poems sound as if she is speaking directly to you.
She uses rhymes to structure her poems.
You could set her poems to music.
She uses repetition to structure her poems.
She makes up her own spellings.
The poems are hard to read out loud.
She uses punctuation to guide the reader.
She uses verse structures.

(b) Now look at examples of the work of other poets in the anthology and try to describe the style of the poet.

Here are some suggestions:
Grace Nichols
    'We the Women', page 14
    'Even Tho', page 26
    'Tropical Death', page 96
Sylvia Plath
    'Stillborn', page 11
    'Blue Moles', page 40
    'Child', page 43
Margaret Atwood
    'Dream 2: Brian the Still-hunter', page 54
    'Charivari', page 56

When you have looked carefully at the styles used by some poets you will see that you can often recognise who has written a particular poem – it has her fingerprints on it. You should be able to describe the style and use quotes from the poems to demonstrate what you are describing.

150

(c) Try this with Ntozake Shange's work. Write an essay with this title; 'Ntozake Shange's poetic style'. Use your notes to help, and make sure you mention all the features of her style you considered in the true or false exercise.

Another way of showing how well you have understood a poet's style and how you 'recognise her fingerprints' is to write 'in the style of' the poet.

(d) Choose a favourite poet and write a poem so like hers in style that someone might mistake it for an original. Put the original and the copy together as a coursework assignment.

Assignment 20: Looking at structures

Poets use the sound patterns they create in their writing to echo or to extend their ideas.

(a) Look through this section and discuss examples of how this is done. Here are some which you should be able to find. Make notes of where you found them:

– the rhythm of a flower opening little by little then stretching out to the sun
– the stress a mother feels when she tries to do ten things at once
– the rhythm of day-to-day life, predictable things happening over and over again
– the soft warm feeling of falling in love
– the rhythm of fast speech
– the rhythm of anger
– a sense of sadness, slow, trudging ordinariness
– the excitement of an incident in the street
– a tight, predictable rhythm echoing a pattern in someone's life which keeps on recurring
– a clock ticking

You will find many other examples if you read the poems carefully and allow the poet's voice to be heard.

151

(b) Use your notes to help you plan an essay entitled 'Sound patterns in a group of poems'.

Here is a topic web to help your planning.

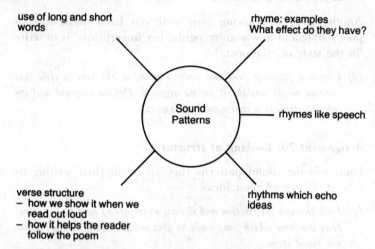

use of long and short words

rhyme: examples
What effect do they have?

Sound Patterns

rhymes like speech

verse structure
– how we show it when we read out loud
– how it helps the reader follow the poem

rhythms which echo ideas

Give examples of each sound pattern you identify. Quote only that bit of the poem which demonstrates the point you are making.

Look back at the study material for Section 1 for help on how to set out quotes (page 136).

Your own writing

The joy and the pain of love have inspired many of the world's greatest poems. It's an emotion we all experience and for each of us it's different. So much has been written about love that it's often hard to find fresh ways of expressing the emotion.

Try writing your own love poems to or about real or imaginary people. Try to make your images startling and fresh. They will be so if you base them on things which are *real* to you.

Look at 'At 3 a.m.', where Wendy Cope sets a scene for sadness. It comes real because she describes the room so vividly. Without the first two verses, the last sad scene would be far less powerful.

Section 4: Moonlongings

Personal response

Assignment 21

These poems have been selected and grouped together because they have one thing in common; each one is based upon one image or a group of images. The pleasure in reading them is in unwinding the image, seeing how skilfully the poet has worked it in, how well it fits and how well it 'wraps up an emotion'.

You can use images like these in poetry or in prose.

Read the poems and discuss their themes and their main images. Then use either the theme or one of the images to spark a piece of your own writing.

For example, in 'Moonlongings':

theme	main moon images
longing for the one you love imagining the one you love writing poems for the one you love	moon – symbol of fertility floating through the sky linking sleepers

Concentrate in your writing on developing the images – using your imagination to make them grow and interconnect.

153

Assignment 22: 'Blue Moles'

The power of these poems lie in their detailed observation of the moles. Sylvia Plath has thought about their lives and deaths and about exactly how they look and move.

Try writing a description of an animal – maybe a pet or a wild creature. In two or three paragraphs of detailed description, make the animal vividly real for the reader.

Assignment 23: 'Not Waving but Drowning'

Stevie Smith says of the man he was

> much too far out all [his] life
> And not waving but drowning.

Often we mistake clowning around for happiness when it really shows sadness. We see it in schools when the class joker is often the person who is most insecure and unhappy.

Use this as an idea for a short story – 'The Tears of the Clown'.

Critical response

Assignment 24: looking at images

Discuss the images in the poem 'Child'.

Your clear eye is the one absolutely beautiful thing.	Why is it clear?
I want to fill it with color and ducks,	Why?
The zoo of the new	What does this mean?
Whose names you meditate – April snowdrop, Indian pipe, Little	How are snowdrops like children?

Stalk without wrinkle,
Pool in which images
Should be grand and classical

How is this like a child?
What does she want the child
to see?

Not this troublous
Wringing of hands, this dark
Ceiling without a star.

Why does she use 'troublous'
rather than 'agitated' or
some other word?
What is the dark ceiling?

Share your discussion with others. You will find a range of interpretations. The poem is very open-ended. It could be about a healthy child or one who is handicapped. It could be about the balance between pain and joy which makes up all our lives.

Assignment 25: 'Not Waving but Drowning'

This poem too isn't quite what it seems at first glance. Read it carefully and discuss what it means.

Assignment 26: 'Blue Moles'

These two poems are fine examples of Sylvia Plath's work. The images are vivid and powerful. Read them out loud and then discuss the images. (Look at the notes on page 115 if you have any difficulty.) Concentrate on the images in italics.

(a) *Think about them and talk them through until you have understood them well enough to explain to another student. Make notes. When you are ready, give the poem to someone who has not read it. Allow her or him time to read it carefully and then explain the images as you understand them.*

(1)
They're out of the *dark's ragbag*, these two
Moles dead in the pebbled rut,
Shapeless as flung gloves, a few feet apart –
Blue suede a dog or fox has chewed

155

One, by himself, seemed pitiable enough,
Little victim unearthed by some large creature
From his *orbit under the elm* root.
The second *carcass* makes a *duel of the affair*:
Blind twins bitten by bad nature.

The sky's far dome is *sane and clear.*
Leaves, undoing their yellow caves
Between the road and the lake water,
Bare no sinister spaces. Already
The *moles look neutral* as the stones.
Their *corkscrew* noses, their *white hands*
Uplifted, stiffen in a family pose.
Difficult to imagine how fury struck –
Dissolved now, smoke of an old war.

(2)
Nightly the battle-shouts start up
In the ear of the *veteran*, and again
I enter the soft pelt of the mole.
Light's death to them: they shrivel in it.
They move through their mute rooms while I sleep,
Palming the earth aside, grubbers
After the fat children of root and rock.
By day, only the topsoil heaves.
Down there one is alone.

Outsize hands prepare a path,
They go before: opening the veins,
Delving for the appendages
Of beetles, sweetbreads, shards – to be eaten
Over and over. And *still the heaven*
Of *final surfeit* is just as far
From the door as ever. What happens between us
Happens in darkness, *vanishes*
Easy and often as each breath.

(b) Write up your notes as an essay entitled 'The imagery of "Blue Moles"'.

Your own writing

Use your imagination!

How many times have you been told to do just that? It's not always easy. Yet your imagination becomes stronger if you exercise it and if you feed it with reading, looking at paintings, listening to music, dancing, drama or whatever creative arts you enjoy. You need to be able to listen to the ideas it throws up and to work them into your writing.

Imagination can't be turned on like a tap and that is why you need to catch the ideas as they arrive.

Many poets carry round a notebook to jot down ideas as they occur to them. Some even keep the notebook by their bed to jot down ideas from dreams before they vanish.

Try keeping a notebook for a few weeks and develop some of the better ideas into poems. You can include the jottings with your poems in your coursework assessment.

Section 5: The planet where they lose things

Personal response

Assignment 27: 'Lost, Never Found'

The Astronomer calls our earth 'the planet where they lose things'. Read the poem carefully and make a list of what the Astronomer has noticed in the 'six million years/Since my promotion to this job'. Even she, watching from the skies, will

157

not have noticed many important things that we have lost – both big and small.

Discuss what our society has lost in your lifetime and that of your parents or what things we may lose in the future. Write about them in an essay called 'The planet where they lose things' or try a poem of your own.

You could use the format of newspaper small advertisements to structure your poem like this:

Lost and Found

Lost   Peace has gone missing
Found   Fear sweeps our streets
          Women walk wary
          Mothers grip their children's hands
          War growls across the world
          Blood gushes on the TV news

Here are some ideas to start with:
   Nuclear War
   AIDS
   Child Abuse
   Racism
   Sexism
   Divorce
   Crime
   Pollution

Assignment 28: 'Two Sketches: Hiroshima, 1945'

People have very different points of view about nuclear weapons. Some say that they have kept the peace in the world. Others say they are so terrible that all countries should disarm, get rid of them. They fear that one day someone will 'press the button' and destroy the world.

   What is your view? Do you know the facts? How can you find out?

158

A good way to do this is by reading all you can about the subjects in a range of newspapers and in your library.

Another way is to write to both the Campaign for Nuclear Disarmament and the Ministry of Defence and ask for material to discuss in class. They have very different points of view and you can compare what they have to say. Your teacher will be able to get videos which show both points of view to help you discuss the issues involved.

Do the research and use the information
– to give a talk as one of your GCSE oral assessments.
– for a class debate. The main speakers in the debate can use their talks as assessment pieces.
– for an essay in which you weigh up the evidence and state your own point of view together with the reasons for holding it.
– for a letter to the government either supporting or attacking their policy.

Assignment 29: 'Charivari' and 'Victims'

(Look at the notes on pages 117–18 for an explanation of 'Charivari' and of some of the difficult words in 'Victims'.)

Margaret Atwood says:

> take care
> to look behind, within
> where the skeleton face beneath
>
> the face puts on its feather mask.

She says that violence and hatred are just beneath the skin and we must

> Resist those cracked
>
> drumbeats. Stop this, Become human.

Think about what happened to the black man in the poem. He was one of millions of people killed because of his race. We don't know the full numbers of black people lynched and murdered in racist attacks. The Ku Klux Klan in America was responsible for many many murders. Millions of Jews were exterminated during the Second World War and their murderers are still being brought to trial. Some, like the Czech boy in 'Victims', survived the concentration camp and still carry the physical and mental scars of that horrific experience. People are being killed in racist attacks today. Racism is part of our history and of our present.

(a) *Read the poems carefully and discuss them. Do your own research on the Holocaust (the murder of millions of Jews) and on the Ku Klux Klan. When you have looked at the evidence of the violence beneath the skin of our society, discuss the following statements. Which do you agree with? Give reasons for your point of view.*

– Everyone is treated equally in our society today.
– There is no racism in our school.
– Young people are less racist than their parents.
– The Ku Klux Klan will never be a powerful movement again.
– There will never be another Holocaust.
– School should not try to change racist attitudes.
– Education cannot change racist attitudes.
– People make too much fuss about racist jokes.

(b) *Use your research and discussion notes*
– *for a class debate on the topic 'Ours is a racist society'.*
– *for an essay on the same topic.*
– *for a poem.*
– *for a short story about a racist incident.*
– *to prepare guidelines as to what your school can and should do to change racist attitudes and prevent racist abuse and attack.*

Assignment 30: 'The Anti-suffragists'

(Look at the notes on page 118 to help you with this poem.)
Charlotte Perkins Gilman was an American writer, poet and

active feminist in the early years of this century when women were fighting for equal rights.

This is a very angry poem. She argues that it was not just men who were unwilling to treat women equally. Many women, too, were anti-suffragists. They argued that women did not need to vote, that things were fine as they were.

Thanks to the work of Charlotte Perkins Gilman and the many women like her who fought for the vote in Britain, women do have equal rights in many ways. We can vote, we can own property, we must be paid the same as men if we do the same work. Is that it? Is there nothing left to fight for?

(a) Discuss this in your group. You could prepare an oral assessment on this theme by:
  – preparing a talk on the topic of equal rights for women.
  – working out a drama improvisation in which a group of people argue about whether women are or should be equal to men.

Here are some ideas to help you research the topic:

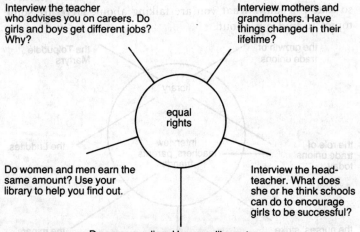

Interview the teacher who advises you on careers. Do girls and boys get different jobs? Why?

Interview mothers and grandmothers. Have things changed in their lifetime?

equal rights

Do women and men earn the same amount? Use your library to help you find out.

Interview the head-teacher. What does she or he think schools can do to encourage girls to be successful?

Do some reading. Use your library to find out about the Suffragists.
(They were also called Suffragettes. Why do you think the name was changed?)

161

Are women still anti-suffragists? Charlotte criticises fashionable women, successful women, religious women, ignorant women, selfish women, and good conscientious women for 'uniting against womanhood'.

(b) Write your own poem on the topic, possibly including all these women.

Assignment 31: 'I Am a Union Woman'

This song is by a remarkable woman. Aunt Molly Jackson married a coal miner when she was only fourteen. She learned to read and write and became a nurse and midwife. Her father, her husband and her son were killed in mining accidents. She was so active in the trade unions that she was forced to leave her home state, Kentucky, in 1931. She spent the rest of her life travelling America, telling people about the miners' conditions and encouraging them to join unions to fight for better wages and conditions.

What is your view about trade unions? Do some research so that you know what you are talking about. Here are some topics to find out about.

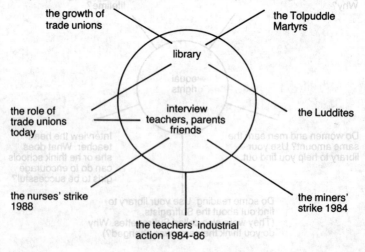

the growth of trade unions

the Tolpuddle Martyrs

library

the role of trade unions today

interview teachers, parents friends

the Luddites

the nurses' strike 1988

the miners' strike 1984

the teachers' industrial action 1984-86

You will find a wide range of opinions about trades unions, whether strikes are acceptable and how workers should improve their pay and conditions.

Use these opinions as the basis for class discussion and an essay entitled: 'Should workers join trade unions?'

Critical response

Assignment 32: What do women write about?

This section has focused on writing about politics and the wider society. How often do you read what *women* have to say about such matters?

(a) Do some research. Here are some ideas to start your enquiries. Does a pattern emerge? Jot down notes about your findings.

(b) Think about what you have discovered and look at the introduction to this anthology. Use what you have learned to discuss the following questions. Try to give examples to demonstrate whether you agree or not.

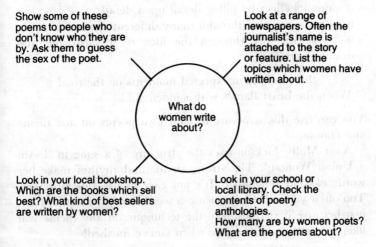

Show some of these poems to people who don't know who they are by. Ask them to guess the sex of the poet.

Look at a range of newspapers. Often the journalist's name is attached to the story or feature. List the topics which women have written about.

What do women write about?

Look in your local bookshop. Which are the books which sell best? What kind of best sellers are written by women?

Look in your school or local library. Check the contents of poetry anthologies.
How many are by women poets? What are the poems about?

163

True or false? Women's writing is:
– not very commercial. Publishers and authors don't make a lot of money from it.
– about very trivial things.
– never about: war, heroic deeds, detectives, police and politics.
– too concerned with love and 'soppy' things.
– not important enough to study.
– not as good as men's writing.
– not as often published as men's writing.

(c) Now use what you have discovered to write an essay with the title: 'Women's Writing'.

Your own writing

Structures

If you re-read 'Lost, Never Found', you will notice its interesting structure:
– it's long
– it gains its effect by piling detail upon detail
– it extends one idea through many different examples
– it works its way through the idea to a surprising and dramatic ending:

    . . . those wholly unexpected moments on the road
  When the heart flames with sudden gold.

You can use this structure in your own poems on any theme you choose.

Aunt Molly Jackson uses the structure of a song in 'I Am a Union Woman'. The strong rhyme and rhythm make her words easy to remember. It's not easy to use this structure. Too often you will find you use a word that is not quite right just because it rhymes. Try the technique on any theme you like. Try setting it to music when you've finished!

Section 6: These mother's bones

Personal response

Assignment 33: 'With Child' and 'For a Child Expected'

Both poems marvel at the creation of a new life, a child who will be herself, a new person whatever the parents want for her.

(a) Read the poems carefully. The notes should help with some of the difficult lines.

Discuss the key ideas in each poem and take notes of your interpretation. Here are some questions to help.

In 'With Child'
– why is the woman 'musing of my own' and 'Big with this loneliness'?
– what is 'Earth's urge' and 'The pure beauty [which] yearns and stirs'?
– why does it turn 'toward stark/And solitary places'?

In 'For a Child Expected'
– why is 'the first flutter' a 'promise of riches to come'?
– how can a baby 'Restore to each the other's lost infancy'?
– what does the writer mean by 'whatever we liked we took'?
– why does the baby 'compel humility'?
– what does she mean by 'May no parental dread or dream/Darken our darling's early beam'?

Now move on from the poems to think about the experiences they describe. (Look at the topic web on page 166.)

Do some reading to help you imagine pregnancy and birth. Your library will contain many books. One very interesting one is *Ourselves and Our Children* (by the Boston Women's Health Collective edited by Michele Cohen and Tina Read). It contains many accounts by parents of their experiences.

165

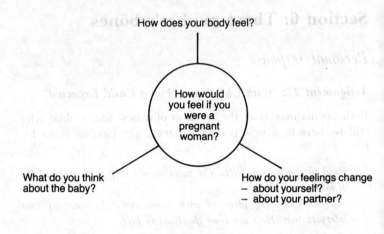

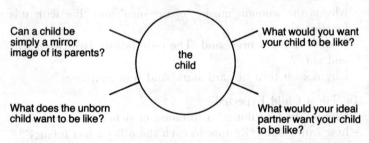

Here are some accounts of pregnancy from the book.

I remember standing at the sink, doing dishes or riding on the subway. I was always trying to imagine what it would be like to have a child. I would try to walk myself through the rituals that everybody knows happen when you have a baby – feeding, washing, dressing, diapering [changing nappies], going for a walk. I wanted to be practised and ready before the actual moment. But it was funny, you can't do that – all I could imagine was this faceless, mild little baby out of an Ivory soap commercial. I think I was trying to get a picture of me as a mother, too. I wanted to know how it would feel to breast-feed, if I could be pleasant waked up in the middle of the night. But the baby and the parent-me were both still embryos.

You think that it's all in your womb and then you find out that your whole life is pregnant.

The biological fact is that it's your wife who is pregnant. The psychological fact, if you admit it to yourself, is that you are too. Becoming a father isn't pocketing a birth certificate, it's moving to a whole new place in life.

At last I feel the equal of my parents. Knowing you are going to have a child is like extending yourself in the world, setting up a tent and saying Here I am, I am important. Now that I'm going to have a child it's like the balance is even. My hand is as rich as theirs, maybe for the first time. I am no longer just a child.

I remember – on the way home from the doctor's – the world made it plain that it was full of parents and children making their way together. In one city block I counted three huge bellies coming toward me – almost like a greeting. And on the subway going home I watched every child I could spot; I felt like I needed to drink in all they could tell me about what was coming. I needed to know what kinds of shoes kids wear, if they can ride the subways by themselves, what a baby sounds like, if they are frightened by crowds and subways. I needed to drink in the parents too – always asking 'Is that how I will be? Is that how I want to be? Is that how my parents were? Is it good? Is it hard?'

I think that carrying a baby inside you is like running as fast as you can. It feels like finally letting go and filling yourself up to the widest limits.

All the time, after I knew Ellie was going to have a baby, I would be in the middle of something else and stop and say 'Hey, man, you made a baby.'

(b) Now you have read these, as well as the poems, develop your own

167

ideas and explore how it might feel to be pregnant and what you might feel about your own child. Choose your own way of writing about it. You may like to write

- a play,
- a poem,
- a letter, from a pregnant woman to her baby's father or from him to her,
- a short story or
- an essay in which you explore your own feelings
- a letter to the unborn child.

Assignment 34: 'The Abortion'

'Somebody who should have been born is gone.' People hold very different views on abortion. Some argue that the baby's life begins at the moment of conception and to abort it is murder. Others say that abortions are acceptable until the time in the pregnancy at which the baby stands a chance of living if it is born. Some people say it is a woman's right to choose whether to continue a pregnancy. Others argue that a society which makes abortion easily available is an uncivilised society because it condones murder. These people want the laws to restrict abortion or make it totally illegal.

What are your views? How much do you already know? Here are some things to find out.

- What are 'back street abortions'?
- What is the law at the moment?
- At what age can a baby have a chance of surviving if it is born too soon?
- What handicaps can be detected before the baby is born?
- How many weeks into the pregnancy can they be detected?
- What is the likely effect on a woman of having an abortion?
- What is the likely effect of having an unwanted child?
- Does the father have any legal rights in the decision-making process?

(a) When you have done the research use what you know to help you

write a short story, a poem, a scene from a play or a letter to a newspaper about the issue.

(b) *People hold very strong views on the subject. You can make a very lively radio documentary programme about it once you have done your basic research. Find people who are able to express a point of view clearly and concisely and interview them on tape. Add your own introduction and conclusion. Try to be unbiased and show both sides of the argument.*

Assignment 35: 'For a Child Born Dead'

When a child is stillborn, its parents suffer greatly. Read the poem and think about the sadness Elizabeth Jennings describes.

Try to imagine the feelings of the mother and perhaps of the midwife who delivers a dead child and use these powerful ideas for a poem, a play or story of your own.

Assignment 36: 'Poem to My Daughter' and 'Transformation'

How much do you know about childbirth? You can read about the process and there are several excellent videos that enable you to witness labour and birth. Every mother has a different birth story to tell.

Try to collect several accounts and write them up. You can put them together as a newspaper article or as a document for another class or group of students to read alongside these poems.

Here are some accounts collected by Sheila Kitzinger in *The Experience of Childbirth* for you to read and discuss:

First baby: I began really to enjoy the birth. It was a wonderful thing to be able to use the power of the contractions to make the baby come. I suppose I have never worked with such a sense of power and assurance of success. . . . A most satisfying and rewarding experience.

169

First baby: It was the most wonderful work, but very hard. My husband soon could see the head. [The nurses felt she should take gas-and-oxygen and placed the mask on her face] but I kept pushing it away, saying, 'No thank you; I have no pain. I have no use for that.' I don't think I would have enjoyed the birth so much with it.

Second baby: It was pain, yes, but without the fear and tension that normally accompanies physical pain. I think my husband felt that too. He said that it was a wonderful experience. We were together in something very real and fundamental. I expect the nurses thought I was quite mad because I kept telling P. that I loved him, and wanting him to kiss me, in between pushes . . .

Assignment 37: 'Emperor Baby'

Read the rest of the poems in this section. There is something wonderful about a new-born baby and these poets try to capture that magic.

Discuss what they have to say. Talk to mothers about how they felt when they looked at their babies. Try your own poem on the topic.

Critical response

Assignment 38: looking at images

Jeni Couzyn has written two of the poems in this section. Both of them are rich in imagery. Look at 'Transformation' and 'Dawn'. Read them first silently and then out loud and discuss the images she uses. Check with the notes on pages 122–3 for any lines you find difficult.

(a) *From the two poems choose five images which you particularly like and discuss with another student why you have chosen them.*

Now go on to read and discuss 'Emperor Baby'. Make notes

170

on the images Jehane Markham uses. Which ones did you find most effective?

(b) Use the notes on both poets to help you plan and write a short essay entitled 'Images of birth and babies in three poems'. Here is a topic web to get you started.

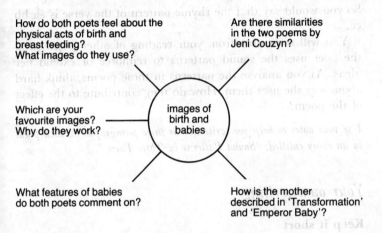

How do both poets feel about the physical acts of birth and breast feeding? What images do they use?

Are there similarities in the two poems by Jeni Couzyn?

Which are your favourite images? Why do they work?

images of birth and babies

What features of babies do both poets comment on?

How is the mother described in 'Transformation' and 'Emperor Baby'?

Assignment 39: looking at structure

Several of these poems use very tightly structured sound patterns.

Read the following poems out loud: 'With Child', 'The Abortion' and 'For a Child Born Dead' and discuss their structure. Look at:

– rhyme patterns
– the length of each line – how many syllables are there?
– repetitions
– rhythm within the lines.

Make notes of your discussion.

There is a simple way to note rhyme patterns. You simply give a letter to each new rhyme like this:

171

> Now I am slow and placid, fond of *sun*,   a
> Like a sleek beast, or a worn *one*,   a
> No slim and languid girl – not *glad*   b
> With the windy trip I once *had*,   b
> But velvet-footed, musing of my *own*,   c
> Torpid, mellow, stupid as a *stone*.   c

So you would say that the rhyme pattern of the verse is aa bb cc.

You will remember from your reading of other poems that the poet uses the sound patterns to reinforce or extend her ideas. As you analyse the patterns in these poems, think hard about *why* she uses them. How do they contribute to the effect of the poem?

Use your notes to help you write two or three paragraphs on each poem in an essay entitled: 'Sound Patterns in Three Poems'.

Your own writing

Keep it short

Sometimes very short poems can be very powerful. Look at 'Her Belly' and 'Being There'. They each explore one idea quickly rather as an artist draws a quick sketch. Try using this technique.

Poems can describe incidents real or imaginary

Look at 'Being There', which describes an event and the poet's thoughts about it, and 'Songs for My Son' which describes how Lorna Goodison attends to her crying child and explores her feelings about him.

You can use this technique. It's a good one to try if you 'can't get started' on a poem. Think of a situation or event that will enable you to explore an idea.

172

Section 7: Heirloom

Personal response

Assignment 40

Often when I am with my daughter I think of my mother, aunts, grandmother. This adds such richness and depth to my relationship with her. It's important for us not to cut ourselves off from our emotional past and take time to miss people – memories of being nurtured sustain me.

Ourselves and Our Children, ed. Michele Cohen and Tina Reed.

This is how one woman reflects on her heirloom, what has been given to her by her mother and what she will pass on to her daughter.

Read these poems about that heirloom and discuss which of the statements below goes with which poem.

- Daughters grow more like their mothers.
- A mother's greatest gift to her child is to share her rich experience of life.
- A mother feels pain as she watches her child become a separate individual.
- The best mothers help their children to leave them.
- The danger of mother love is that the mother's own life gets swallowed up in that of her children.
- Daughters need to know about their mothers' lives. They respect them and feel sorrow for their pain.

Assignment 41

When you have read this section and the previous section, 'These mother's bones', think about motherhood. Think about the experience of birth and of seeing your child grow up and grow away from you.

173

Write about how you imagine the experience of motherhood would feel to you or to an imaginary person. Write
– a poem
– a play
– a short story.

Assignment 42

Use these poems as a way of getting mothers (possibly your own) to talk about their experience of motherhood and their feelings about their own mothers.

Choose four poems to read to the mothers you have chosen to interview. Work out a few questions to get them talking. Think whether you are going to take notes or use a cassette recorder to tape the interview.

Use your interviews as the basis for
– a talk as an oral assessment
– an essay: 'The experience of motherhood'
– a newspaper feature entitled 'Mothers Talking'
– a short story or play
– a conversation with your own parents or guardians.

Critical response

Assignment 43: the poet as storyteller

Several poems in this anthology tell a story or describe an event which has a big effect on the poet.

Read 'For My Mother's Mother' and 'Pain for a Daughter' in this section. Then go on to read two poems by Grace Nichols on pages 103 and 104: 'Taint' and 'Ala'.

The power in each poem comes from its account of a time of pain in a woman's life. The poets make us share in that pain, be part of that story. Consider how the poet tells her story and how she involves us in it.

174

Does she use images?
– many?
– few?
– what effect do they have?
What structure does she use?
– verses?
– rhymes?
– rhythm patterns?
– repetitions?
What are the most striking lines in each poem? Why?
Which is the most powerful story?

When you have made notes on these questions you can use them as the basis for an essay: 'The poet as storyteller'.

Assignment 44: the poet as letter writer

Read 'Mama' in this section and 'night letter' on page 28. Both poets use the format of a letter to shape their poems. It is very useful because it makes the reader feel as if the letter is addressed directly to her or him; as if the reader is Mama or the faithless lover.

Try the technique. Write a poem/letter on the same topic as 'Mama' or 'night letter' and use the same style as far as possible. If you do this well your poem will show that you understand and appreciate the original poem and so can be used as a piece of coursework.

Assignment 45: 'Heirloom'

'Heirloom' is a superb poem. It is powerful although its subject is very simple. It is very finely crafted. Read it and discuss it carefully and use your notes to write a critical appreciation of it.

Here are some ideas to help you.

COURSEWORK ASSIGNMENTS: SECTION BY SECTION

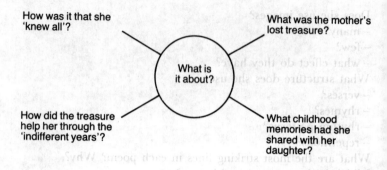

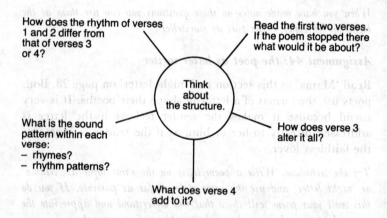

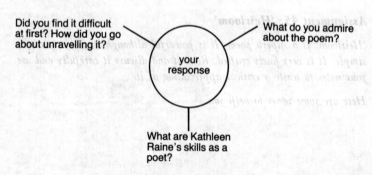

176

Your own writing

What should poetry be about?

Poetry can be about almost anything, but we tend to use this very intense form of writing for powerful and intense emotions or experiences. It works very well when you are trying to describe something outside the ordinary run-of-the-mill experience. Good examples from this section are:

– the mother who 'saw the living skein/Of which the world is woven'
– the daughter who recognised 'this sameness/that I see'
– the moment at which:

> I saw her torn in childbirth,
> and I saw her, at that moment,
> in her own death and I knew that she
> knew

– the sudden understanding:

> what was her name?
> Judith, she said.
> I named my first daughter after my mother.

You can use your own poetry to explore experiences like this which happen to you or to those close to you. You may only have to read about an experience to want to write about it. Try to write your best poetry when you want to express experiences or emotions which are powerful and important to you.

Section 8: You can wear terrible shirts and grow more fat

Personal response

Assignment 46: 'The Second Wife'

'She hears him sigh, old Aprils in his face.' The second wife fears that her husband sometimes longs for the sweetness and the passion of first love. Discuss her fear:

– Does love change with age?

– Can you ever love again as passionately as your first love?

Here are some true or false questions which should help your discussion.

True or false?

First love is always the best.

When you're young you don't understand real love.

People always yearn for 'romance'.

Living with someone, day in, day out can kill romantic love.

The second wife will always be second best.

Women and men's experiences of love are the same.

The best basis for love is true friendship.

You can write your discussion in any way you like. You may find you have sparked off some ideas which could develop into poems or short stories.

Assignment 47: 'Elizabeth Gone'

This section also includes poems about death. Read 'Elizabeth Gone' and discuss what the poet tells you about death and about her feelings.

How will your death be? We know as little of our deaths as we remember of our births. We all have our hopes and fears about death and they are often painful to explore.

Use these poems to help you talk and write about death. Use whatever format for your writing you choose: poem, play, story or essay.

Assignment 48: 'Tropical Death'

Read 'Tropical Death' to see how Grace Nichols' 'fat black woman' wants to go. She wants a 'nine-night wake' and 'some bawl'. What kind of funeral, what kind of saying goodbye would you wish for? Do some research in your library about funeral rituals in different cultures. Which match most closely what you would like? Try not simply to opt for the ritual you know and feel is familiar to you.

Write it up as a story, play, poem or essay.

Critical response

Assignment 49

Which is the best poem in this section? Read the poems carefully and choose which you think is the most powerful. Then write an essay giving reasons for your choice.

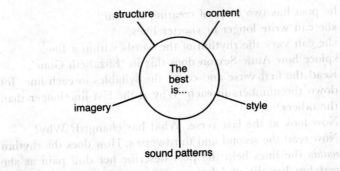

Assignment 50: looking at structure

The poem 'The Second Wife' is a sonnet. This format has been used for hundreds of years by many great poets including

Milton, Petrarch and Shakespeare. They each had their own particular version of the form and this one is of the Shakespearian variety.

How do you recognise a sonnet? It has:
– fourteen lines
– a particular rhyme pattern
– roughly ten syllables in each line

What rhyme patterns can sonnet writers use? They can invent their own or use:

Shakespeare's	abab	cdcd	effe gg
Milton's	abbaabba	cdccdc	
Petrarch's	abab	abab	cdcdgg

Shakespeare's pattern is very attractive because it builds up an idea in three equal sections and then turns it upside down in the last two lines. Look again at 'The Second Wife' to see how it works.

It's a difficult form to copy because it is very strict, but it's well worth trying if you are prepared to work at it. Try composing a sonnet on any theme for a coursework assignment.

Assignment 51: looking at rhythm

The poet has two ways of creating rhythm:
– she can write longer or shorter lines,
– she can vary the rhythm of the words within a line.

Explore how Anne Sexton does this in 'Elizabeth Gone'.

– Read the first verse and count the syllables in each line. Jot down the numbers in each. Why is the last line longer than the others?
– Now look at the last verse. What has changed? Why?
– Now read the second and third verses. How does the rhythm *within* the lines help the poet describe her dull pain as she watches her die and her emptiness and sharp pain as she receives her ashes?
– Now go on to the last verse. How does the rhythm change as she accepts her death and rejoices in her life?

If you have worked this through carefully you will be able to write a short essay on the rhythm of 'Elizabeth Gone'.

Assignment 52: looking at images

Sometimes a whole poem can be built on one idea. Look at 'Skins' by Judith Wright. You may need to use the notes to help you with a few ideas. Read the poem carefully and discuss with a friend how the poet explores one key image.

Compare this with 'Elizabeth Gone' and the rich range of images Anne Sexton uses.

Here are some questions about the poem to help you focus on the images. Make notes on your discussion.

– In the first verse, how are the ideas of 'nest' and 'baby' linked?
– In the second verse, why was 'nest' changed to 'crate'?
– How are the words 'clay' and 'mask' linked to 'crate'?
– What do the words 'satin' and 'suede' remind you of?
– In the third verse, what does the phrase 'stones that their oven had blest' mean?
– What does the phrase 'cathedral of spells' mean?
– In the last verse, how are the words 'apple' and 'August' linked?
– What does the use of the word 'crèche' mean? Does it fit with the idea of death?

Using 'Elizabeth Gone' and 'Skins' or any of the poems in this section write an essay entitled 'Images of old age and death'.

Your own writing

The big issues

You can and should use your poetry to explore ideas which are very important to people. Death is just such an issue. People are often afraid to think about it or talk about it and yet it is the one certain thing in all our lives – we will die.

You may have touched death. You may have lost someone close to you or even been in danger of death yourself. It can often help you deal with grief and fear to write about your emotions and experience. You do not need to show people poems that are very personal. Not everything should be put into GCSE coursework!

Developing techniques

If you tried to write a sonnet after reading 'The Second Wife' you will know that it is a difficult form to use. It may not immediately suit what you want to say. However, it is very important to practise different forms and to develop skills that way. Your poetry develops just as a painter's skill develops, by:

– training yourself to observe life closely so you can describe it in words
– getting better and better in a range of techniques so that you can choose which one best fits what you have to say.

Section 9: A woman undaunted

Personal response

Assignment 53

This section celebrates how women find ways to survive and sometimes to be happy. It celebrates the wish to be, as Grace Nichols says, 'a woman/holding my beads in my hand', a woman in control.

(a) *Read the poems and discuss how women 'take control' in each of them.*

(b) Try to fit the following statements to the poems. Which goes with which?

– Surviving means accepting and living with pain.
– Above all else, a woman wants to have dignity and to make her own decisions.
– Women's skills of managing homes and families are often undervalued.
– Death is better than slavery.
– To be happy a woman must make the best of what's available to her.
– Women learn strength from other women.
– Women help each other to take control of their lives.
– To be happy, a woman must refuse to accept second best.
– You have to take risks to be free and happy.

Assignment 54: 'Taint' and 'Ala'

Look at these two powerful poems by Grace Nichols. Find out more about slavery by researching in your library. Read everything you can. Try Toni Morrison's novel *The Beloved* which is about a woman slave killing her baby to set her free from slavery.

Present what you have found out as: a talk (to your class or to another group), an essay, a play or a poem.

Some ways of writing imaginatively about slavery could be:
– letters from a mother to her children sold away from her. She may not know where they are but writes letters just to unburden her feelings.
– a short story based on 'Ala'.
– a newspaper article written as if you witnessed either the capture of a number of slaves or the execution of the women in 'Ala'.
– a play in which one slave tries to persuade the mother not to kill the baby.

Assignment 55: 'Lineage' and 'An Even Shape'

A lot of the world's great writing celebrates the heroic, public deeds of men. They fight and conquer, discover new lands, rule countries, change the world. Women have usually been invisible, except for Boadicea and Queen Elizabeth I! Increasingly women are playing a full part in public life and their achievements are being recognised. However, we don't always pay tribute to the huge contribution women make to society.

Margaret Walker's grandmothers in 'Lineage' 'followed plows and bent to toil'. Women in the Third World still do. Women have made the land fertile and have made houses into homes. Look at the achievement of the woman in 'An Even Shape'. She will never make the history books like the generations of women before her, but she deserves the recognition of this poem.

Think about a woman in everyday life whom you respect. What are her skills, her special qualities? Write a poem or story to celebrate her achievement. Remember Margaret Walker's grandmothers. 'They were full of sturdiness and singing.'

Assignment 56: 'get it & feel good'

Read the poem out loud and discuss Ntozake Shange's advice. Have you found that 'what's available/cd add up in the long run'?

What advice would you give to someone of your age who wanted to be happy? What should she/he do? Try it as a poem or letter.

Critical response

Assignment 57: looking at the work of one poet

There are three poems by Grace Nichols here. You will find three more in this anthology: 'We the Women', page 14, 'Even

Tho', page 26, and 'Tropical Death', page 96. Read all six and consider what they have in common. Here are some headings for you to use for your notes.

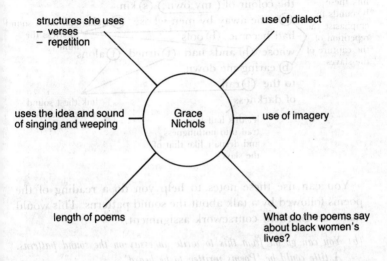

There may be several other points you would want to consider.

Use your notes and relevant quotes to write an essay on Grace Nichols' poems. If you want to read more of her work you will find details of her publications in the Wider Reading section of this study material.

Assignment 58: hearing the sound of poems

Most of these poems work best when they are read aloud. Which do you think are written to be heard? Try them all and choose three which work especially well. Practise reading them aloud until you feel that you are allowing the words to be heard and the sound patterns to emerge.

(a) Now write notes to go with each of your three poems to help someone else read them well. Here is an example of notes to go with 'Taint'.

185

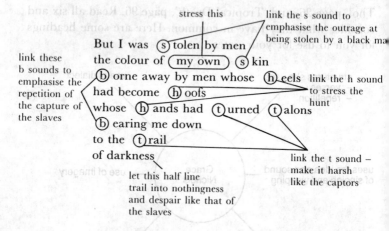

stress this

link the s sound to emphasise the outrage at being stolen by a black ma

But I was ⓢtolen by men the colour of (my own) ⓢkin

link these b sounds to emphasise the repetition of the capture of the slaves

ⓑorne away by men whose ⓗeels had become ⓗoofs whose ⓗands had ⓣurned ⓣalons ⓑearing me down to the ⓣrail of darkness

link the h sound to stress the hunt

let this half line trail into nothingness and despair like that of the slaves

link the t sound – make it harsh like the captors

You can use these notes to help you do a reading of the poems followed by a talk about the sound patterns. This would make an excellent coursework assignment.

(b) You can go on from this to write an essay on the sound patterns. A title could be 'Poems written to be heard'.

Your own writing

Where do poems come from?

These poems of anger, pain and, most of all, celebration of women's ability to survive 'undaunted' are all written by black women and are based on what they know happened to women like them in the past or on their experience of trying to survive here and now.

Some are about dramatic events, shocking and terrifying. Some are about ordinary, everyday happiness. You can write about both.

Often the very best poems are those based on your own personal experience and observation of everyday life. You can and should use your daily life as the basis for writing. You need to develop the skills of expressing what it is you see and hear and feel.

When you can make things 'feel real' in your poems, then you can start to write about events that you have not experienced personally. Notice how Grace Nichols makes us believe that she was one of the women watching the execution of the 'rebel woman'. She makes us feel 'the soft mould' of the baby's head and 'the slow and painful picking away of the flesh'.

Your observations of daily life do not always have to be worked into full-blown poems. Your notebook is the place to store jottings, the beginnings of an idea that you will call upon when you have a place for it in a poem.

Assignments based on the whole anthology

Assignment 1

How would you introduce this anthology to another class? It's likely that another group may be studying it at the same time as or after your group. Discuss how you would present it to them. Would you:
– talk about it first or start off with a poem?
– discuss why it's worth studying an anthology of poems by women?
– recommend certain sections or poems?
– take examples of work you have done?
  This could be an oral coursework assignment and later could develop into a piece of written work.

Assignment 2

Poems are sound pictures. Plan a poetry reading based on this anthology. Can you visit another group, get an audience in assembly or invite parents to an evening performance? Bearing in mind the time available, select poems which are best read aloud. Practise reading them to do them justice. It might be helpful to prepare a 'handout' for your audience giving them
– titles
– names of poets
– names of who is to read each one
– notes to help them understand the poems where necessary
– notes as to why you particularly like each poem.

Assignment 3

Choose your own favourites and make them yours. If you enjoy a particular poem keep a copy of it in the notes you make on the anthology so you can return to it again and again. Learn it off by heart if you really enjoy it, then you can call it to mind whenever you want. Learning poems is very enjoyable and it enables you to have many, many poets' voices available to help you in your own writing.

Assignment 4

Make this into a piece of coursework. Choose a group of your favourite poems and write a critical appreciation of them. Look at

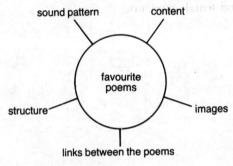

Choose groups, such as poems
– by the same writer
– on a similar theme
– using similar techniques.

Assignment 5

Use the sections in the anthology to help you organise an assignment.
(a) In groups plan a reading and discussion of one section.
(b) Choose your favourite section and write a critical appreciation of it.
(c) Argue about the groupings of poems.
(d) Choose six poems to make up a new section. Identify a key idea to link them.

(e) Write a few paragraphs explaining how your section has been organised.

(f) You can go on to suggest coursework assignments based on your new section.

Assignment 6

Use all your notes and thoughts on the anthology to help you write a letter either to your local examination board or a major publisher saying why you think more women's poetry should be made available to GCSE students and should be studied by male and female students.

Wider reading

Many of the poets in this anthology have published volumes of their own poetry. Here are some you may enjoy:

Margaret Atwood, *The Journals of Susanna Moodie* (Oxford University Press).
You may also enjoy her novels. Try *The Edible Woman* (Virago).

Wendy Cope, *Making Cocoa for Kingsley Amis* (Faber and Faber).

Lorna Goodison, *Tamarind Season* (Humming bird); *I am becoming my mother* (New Beacon Books).

Grace Nichols, *A Dangerous Knowing: Four black women poets* (Sheba Feminist Publishers); *The Fat Black Woman's Poems* (Virago); *i is a long memoried woman* (Caribbean Cultural International).

Marge Piercy, *Breaking Camp* (Wesleyan University Press).
You may also enjoy her novels. Try *Woman at the Edge of Time* (Virago).

Sylvia Plath, *Collected Poems. (Faber and Faber).*
There are smaller volumes of her poems too.

Ntozake Shange, *Nappy Changes* (Bantam Books); *For colored girls who have considered suicide when the rainbow is enuf* (Eyre Methuen).

Alice Walker, *Horses make a landscape look more beautiful* (Women's Press).
You may also enjoy her superb novel *The Colour Purple* (Virago).

There are several excellent anthologies of women poets. Here are some to read:
In the Pink (Women's Press).

No Holds Barred (Women's Press).

The Bloodaxe Book of Contemporary Women Poets: Eleven British Writers, ed. Jeni Couzyn (Bloodaxe).

The World Split Open: Women Poets 1552–1950, ed. Louise Bernikow (Women's Press).

Watchers and Seekers: Creative Writing by Black Women in Britain, ed. Cobham & Collins (Women's Press).

Assignments based on wider reading

Assignment 1: looking at the work of one poet

As you read a volume of writing by one poet, her style, her concerns, her view of the world and the images she uses to share that view become clear. Reflect on your reading doing the following:

(a) Write a review of the anthology as if you were a news-paper reviewer. Consider the poet's strengths and weak-nesses. Were there any poems which simply did not work? Quote from the poems to give the reader a taste of the poet's style and concerns.

(b) Write a critical appreciation of a group of poems. Here you would examine the poems in much more detail.

(c) Write a poem of your own 'in the style of' your chosen poet.

(d) Prepare a lesson for your class on the poet. You will need to make sure that you have copies of the poems. What do you want the class to focus on? How will you get them involved?

Assignment 2: thinking about women's writing

You may well have done some work on this as part of your work in the Critical Response section for 'The planet where they lose things' (page 163). If you have read more widely you will be able to extend that work. You could write an essay entitled 'Women's Writing'. Choose three or four poets to discuss and use their work to show the range of topics women writers consider. Use your essay to give your own view as to whether:

– 'women's issues' are only of interest to women
– women only write about 'women's issues'.

Assignment 3

Select poems by your favourite writers for a reading to an audience such as your class, an assembly, an audience of parents, an audience of the general public or your local radio station.

If a group of you do this then each could read poems by a particular poet or on a particular theme.

Assignment 4

Think about themes in poems you have enjoyed and write about how different writers explore them. Some themes might be birth, death, finding your way in life, love, politics, friendship, childhood or anger.

Acknowledgements

We are grateful to the following for permission to reproduce copyright material:

Angus & Robertson (UK) and Virago Press for the poems 'Skins' and 'Victims' from *Phantom Dwelling* by Judith Wright, Copyright © Judith Wright 1985; Associated Book Publishers (UK) Ltd for the poems 'lady in blue' by Ntozake Shange from *For colored girls who have considered suicide when the rainbow is enuf* and 'night letter' and 'get it & feel good' by Ntozake Shange from *Nappy edges* (pub. Methuen London); the author, Patricia Beer for her poem 'The Fifth Sense'; Bloodaxe Books Ltd for the poems 'Dawn', 'Transformation' and 'House of Change' from *Life by Drowning: Selected Poems* edited by Jeni Couzyn (pub. Bloodaxe Books 1985); Caribbean Cultural International for the poems 'Ala', 'Taint' and 'Holding My Beads' by Grace Nichols from *i is a long memoried woman* (pub. 1983); the author, Merle Collins for her poem 'No Dialects Please' Copyright © Merle Collins, from *Watchers and Seekers* ed. Rhonda Cobham and Merle Collins (pub. Women's Press 1987); the author, Christine Craig for her poem 'An Even Shape' from *Jamaica Woman* ed. P. Mordecai and M. Morris; the author, Jean D'Costa for her poem 'Lost, Never Found'; the author, Anna Dölezal for her poem 'To Friends'; Faber & Faber Ltd for the poems 'Rondeau Redoublé' and 'At 3 a.m.' from *Making Cocoa for Kingsley Amis* by Wendy Cope and 'For a child expected' from *The Nine Bright Shiners* by Anne Ridler; the author, Ruth Fainlight for her poem 'It Must'; Kalli Halvorson on behalf of the author Susan Griffin, for her poems 'Three Poems for Women and 'Love Should Grow Up Like a Wild Iris in the Field'; Henry Holt & Co, Inc for the poem 'The Second Wife' from *White April* by Lizette Woodworth Reese. Copyright 1930 by Lizette Woodworth Reese and renewed 1958 by A. Austin Dietrich; Institute of Jamaica Publications Ltd for the poems 'I'm in Here Hiding' and

'Moonlongings' from *Tamarind Season* by Lorna Goodison © Lorna Goodison 1980; the author's agents for the poems 'For a Child Born Dead' and 'Old Woman' from *Collected Poems* by Elizabeth Jennings (pub. Macmillan); the author's agents for the poem 'Dawn Walker' by Jenny Joseph (c) Jenny Joseph from *The Bloodaxe Book of Contemporary Women Poets* ed. J Couzyn (pub. Bloodaxe Books 1985); the author, Margot Jordan for her poem 'Silence is Nearer to Truth'; Marcia D. Liles on behalf of the estate of Genevieve Taggard, for the poem 'With Child' from *Collected Poems: 1918–1938* by Genevieve Taggard (pub. Harper & Brothers 1938) Copyright 1938, renewed 1966; the executor James MacGibbon, for the poem 'Not Waving but Drowning' by Stevie Smith from *The Collected Poems of Stevie Smith* (Penguin Modern Classics); the author, Jehane Markham for her poem 'Emperor Baby'; the author, Felicity Napier for her poem 'Blinis'; New Beacon Books Ltd for the poem 'Songs for my Son' from *I Am Becoming My Mother* by Lorna Goodison (pub. New Beacon Books Ltd 1986); the author, Grace Nichols for her poems 'Even Tho' and 'We the Women'; Oxford University Press Canada for the poems 'Dream 2: Brian the Still-hunter' and 'Charivari' from *The Journals of Susanna Moodie* by Margaret Atwood; the author's agents for the poem 'The Woman in the Ordinary' by Marge Piercy; the author's agent for the poems 'Stillborn', 'Blue Moles' and 'Child' from *Collected Poems* by Sylvia Plath, Copyright Ted Hughes 1965, 1967, 1981 (pub. Faber & Faber Ltd); the author, Ethel Portnoy for her poem 'Being There'; the author, Rita Anyiam-St John for her poem 'Mama'; the author's agents for the poems 'Elizabeth Gone' and 'The Abortion' from *Selected Poems* by Anne Sexton (pub. Oxford University Press) and 'Pain for a Daughter' from *Live or Die* by Anne Sexton Copyright © 1966 Anne Sexton (pub. Houghton Mifflin 1966); the author, Anne Stevenson for her poem 'The Mother' Copyright Anne Stevenson; the author and Oxford University Press for the poem 'Poem to My Daughter' from *Minute by Glass Minute* by Anne Stevenson © Anne Stevenson

1982 (pub. 1982); Unwin & Hyman Ltd for the poem 'Heirloom' from *Collected Poems* by Kathleen Raine (pub. Allen & Unwin); Virago Press for the poems 'Hiroshima 1945' from *Beginning the Avocado* by Gillian Allnut, Copyright © Gillian Allnut 1987 and 'Tropical Death' by Grace Nichols from *The Fat Black Woman's Poems* (pub. Virago); the author's agents for the poems 'How Poems Are Made/A Discredited View' and 'Mississippi Winter IV' from *Horses Make a Landscape Look More Beautiful* by Alice Walker (pub. The Women's Press); The Women's Press Ltd for the poem 'Her Belly' by Anna 'Swir' © Anna Swirszczynska, English trans © Grazyna Baran and Margaret Marshmen 1985, from *No Holds Barred* ed. The Raving Beauties (pub. The Womens Press Ltd).

We have been unable to trace the copyright holders in the following poems and would appreciate any information that would enable us to do so:

'Lineage' by Margaret Walker Alexander; 'For My Mother's Mother' by Judith McDaniel and 'Ye Housewyf' by Meg Wanless.

Longman Study Texts   **General editor: Richard Adams**

Novels and stories

Jane Austen
  Emma
  Pride and Prejudice
Charlotte Brontë
  Jane Eyre
Emily Brontë
  Wuthering Heights
Charles Dickens
  Great Expectations
  Oliver Twist
George Eliot
  The Mill on the Floss
  Silas Marner
Nadine Gordimer
  July's People
Thomas Hardy
  Far from the Madding Crowd
  The Mayor of Casterbridge
Aldous Huxley
  Brave New World
Robin Jenkins
  The Cone-Gatherers
D H Lawrence
  Sons and Lovers
Somerset Maugham
  Short Stories
John Mortimer
  Paradise Postponed
George Orwell
  Animal Farm
  Nineteen Eighty-Four
Alan Paton
  Cry, The Beloved Country
Paul Scott
  Staying On
Mark Twain
  The Adventures of Huckleberry Finn
H G Wells
  The History of Mr Polly
Virginia Woolf
  To be Lighthouse

Plays

Alan Ayckbourn
  Absurd Person Singular
  Sisterly Feelings
Oliver Goldsmith
  She Stoops to Conquer
Ben Jonson
  Volpone
Christopher Marlowe
  Doctor Faustus
J B Priestley
  An Inspector Calls
Terence Rattigan
  The Winslow Boy
Willy Russell
  Educating Rita
Peter Shaffer
  Amadeus
  Equus
  The Royal Hunt of the Sun
William Shakespeare
  Macbeth
  The Merchant of Venice
  Romeo and Juliet
Bernard Shaw
  Androcles and the Lion
  Arms and the Man
  Caesar and Cleopatra
  The Devil's Disciple
  Major Barbara
  Pygmalion
  Saint Joan
Richard Brinsley Sheridan
  The Rivals
  The School for Scandal
John Webster
  The Duchess of Malfi
  The White Devil
Oscar Wilde
  The Importance of Being Earnest

Editor: George MacBeth
  Poetry for Today
Editor: Michael Marland
  Short Stories for Today